Contra Mundum
Joseph de Maistre & the Birth of Tradition

THOMAS GARRETT ISHAM

Contra Mundum

Joseph de Maistre
&
The Birth of Tradition

ANGELICO PRESS
SOPHIA PERENNIS

First published in the USA
by Angelico Press/Sophia Perennis 2017
© Thomas Garrett Isham 2017

Series editor: James R. Wetmore

For information, address:
Angelico Press
4709 Briar Knoll Dr.
Kettering, OH 45429
angelicopress.com
info@angelicopress.com

ISBN 978 1 62138 250 8 pb
ISBN 978 1 62138 251 5 cloth
ISBN 978 1 62138 252 2 ebook

Cover design: Michael Schrauzer

CONTENTS

Introduction: One Tradition, Two Lives 1

1   The Life and the Doctrine 7

2   Theosophy and Its Compensations 25

3   Maistre Among the Masons 35

4   Maistre and the Counter-Enlightenment 47

5   Maistre and the Catholic-Protestant Split 63

6   Joseph de Maistre and America 79

7   Tradition and Modernity 91

8   Maistre's Relevance for Today 103

   Appendix I: Maistre and Isaiah Berlin 119

   Appendix II: Tradition in the Protestant World 127

   Bibliography 137

   Index of Names 141

To Ava Rose, Gareth James, and Gabriel Moon:

May you love the permanent things.

Introduction
One Tradition, Two Lives

BEFORE René Guénon, there was Joseph de Maistre. One tradition, two lives. One tradition, two ways of living it, teaching it, bequeathing it.

To those who have heard of him, Joseph de Maistre is the Ur-Traditionalist of the early modern age. Defender of throne and altar, theorist of Continental conservatism, foe of the French Revolution; this scion of old Savoy is typecast as the unbending advocate of the old order and the near pathological opponent of the new. He is notorious as a chilling student of violence and sacrifice, as a defender of the hangman, as the advocate of papal power.

What is less known of this orthodox churchman and conservative moralist—or largely ignored when it is known—is Maistre's deep and abiding devotion to esoteric theory and practice, to his immersion in the illuminist and theosophical currents that simmered beneath both radical and traditional orthodoxies in the late eighteenth and early nineteenth centuries. His social and political theories, his ultramontane Catholicism, and his reputation as a founder of modern, self-conscious conservatism, were each in turn influenced by the esoteric[1] currents that leavened his otherwise austere

---

1. Although the term "esotericism" did not exist in Maistre's day, the phenomena it represented most certainly did. It was first used as a noun—*l'ésotérisme*—by Jacques Matter in his 1828 *Histoire du gnosticisme*. The term was popularized in the 1850s by the occultist and ceremonial magician Eliphas Lévi. Derived from the ancient Greek adjective *esôterikôs*, it referred initially to hidden spiritual teachings or "mysteries," reserved for the elite but hidden from the masses. Closer to our own day it has come to categorize forms of knowledge such as alchemy, astrology, magic, and related "sacred sciences." In Maistre's time, it was distinct from both Enlightenment Rationalism and historic Christianity, competing orthodoxies of the eighteenth and nineteenth centuries. Though the term is anachronistic in regard to Maistre, we use it for convenience in referring to the phenomena cited above.

doctrine. Thus Maistre's conservatism, seminal to this day in certain varieties of traditionalist and rightist thought, is enriched by a variety of unlikely influences, ranging from alchemy to Alexandrian Christianity, from Freemasonry to Neo-Platonism. In brief, it is linked to the theosophical[2] stream of quest and speculation that has for so long irrigated the subterranean levels of Western thought.

In expounding Maistre and his ideas, we will allude frequently to the comparable principles of a more recent figure, René Guénon (1886–1951). We shall not conflate the two men or their ideas, for in some ways they were quite unlike one another, *sui generis* in spite of a like-minded allegiance to perennial philosophy,[3] with its universal and immutable principles. Nor was Guénon an extensive borrower of Maistre's ideas and sources; the two simply discovered and expounded in their highly individual ways a living, breathing traditional doctrine that converged at many points and that bears examination and comparison.

Neither savant is widely known to the public, though Maistre (1753–1821) is familiar to historians of ideas, especially conservative ideas and especially in Europe. Awareness is now growing beyond such confines, however, as earlier neglect in English-speaking countries gives way to widening attention by the academy, and deservedly so. For Maistre's masterly prose and profound and provocative

2. Theosophy—"Wisdom of God"—derives from the Greek *theosophia* and is part of the broader field of esotericism. In early Christianity, several Latin and Greek Church Fathers used it as a synonym for theology. By the Renaissance, it began to take on gnostic coloration, and in subsequent centuries developed into a knowledge of the relations between God, humanity, and the universe. It seeks to reintegrate the self into relationship with the various levels of reality, creating a unitive vision encompassing nature and supernature.

3. Perennial philosophy holds that each of the world's religious traditions reflects a single, universal truth on which are built the outer or exoteric expressions of the individual faiths. The term was coined by Agostino Steuco (1497–1558), who drew on the fifteenth century Neo-Platonism of Marsilio Ficino and Giovanni Pico Della Mirandola. Maistre cannot be classified as a thorough-going perennialist but his metaphysical and theological views were heavily influenced by such a point of view and largely comfortable with it. Guénon, perennialist though he was, insisted emphatically on the practice of a single religion, rejecting as he did any form of syncretism. As a Roman Catholic, Maistre practiced the Catholic religion while informed about and appreciative of other religions.

observations make of him the Continental counterpart to Edmund Burke (1729–1797), the Anglo-Irish founder of British conservatism and a thinker greatly admired by Maistre himself. Both men developed conservative themes and ideas in response to the violence and follies of the French Revolution, but it was Maistre, owing to his greater metaphysical depth, who did so in the context of what we have termed the perennial philosophy. Moreover, Burke was a Whig, albeit a chastened and conservative one, whereas Maistre, despite early flirtations with reform ideas of a modernist tint, found his Archimedean point in a conservatism rooted in deeper strata. Burke, the prudent and practical statesman, relied heavily on utilitarian and empirical arguments to make his case and advance his cause, whereas the more radical Maistre relied on providentialist, metaphysical, and sociological arguments in crafting his broader perennial positions.

Setting Burke aside, we turn to the commonalities between Maistre and Guénon, which are of particular interest here. We can identify several of them. Both men, for example, were enthusiasts of Freemasonry and its social and religious possibilities; both explored the domain of sacred science and its continuing significance; both investigated esoteric teachings and engaged in esoteric disciplines; both discerned a metaphysical unity beneath the varied expressions of religion; both refused to subordinate religious truth to the latest claims of natural science; both were alienated from the elite shibboleths of their day; and both left their native lands for a life of exile.

There were differences, too. Though a metaphysical thinker, Maistre engaged passionately in the political sphere, both as theorist and partisan. This Guénon did not do, though he was a frequent commentator on public issues more broadly. (His calling was instead to serve as the prolific formulator of the traditionalist school, a body of thought that continues to bear fruit not only in Europe but in America, with a numerically modest but growing number of followers.) Though both men were devoutly religious, Maistre was a Roman Catholic and Guénon a Muslim convert (though he was raised a Roman Catholic). Though both wrote in French, they differed greatly in style. Thus in Guénon one finds a precise, largely abstract, almost mathematical form of expression, elegant and beautiful after its own fashion. In contrast, Maistre's style—though every bit as lucid as Guénon's—was lyrical and picturesque, alive with color and metaphor, earning its author a reputation as a master of prose. Despite these differences, both were powerful writers, superb communicators of first principles and their implications.

As observed earlier, Maistre's work—and critiques of it—have of late been appearing more frequently in English translation. Thus his audience on this side of the Atlantic, as well as in Britain, is growing. While he has been long familiar to serious readers on the Continent, both to those who love him and to those who hate him (but who nonetheless enjoy his incomparable prose style), American and British readers are discovering that this champion of throne and altar is worth listening to. Regardless of one's personal convictions or nationality, Maistre's perennial principles and shrewd analysis of human nature make him an important observer of religious, philosophical, and historical developments.

He is especially important owing to his strategic location in time and place, for it enabled him to observe and analyze the first modern, ideological revolution as it unfolded next door to his native Savoy (a province of the Kingdom of Piedmont-Sardinia until 1792, at which time it was invaded and annexed by armies of the First French Republic). Though driven into exile, he continued to monitor the Revolution from afar as it propelled itself from one crisis to the next. In 1797, he published *Considérations sur la France* (*Considerations on France*), the work that established his literary and political reputation. In that insightful study, he paid homage to France as a nation with a divine mission, as "the head of the religious system" of Europe and as the benefactor of civilization generally. But he believed it a mission betrayed. Rather than fulfill its destiny, the *Ancien Régime*—monarchy, aristocracy, and clergy—had indulged the doctrines of the *philosophes*, the public intellectuals of Enlightenment who sowed the seeds of atheism and materialism in a variety of fields. According to Maistre, the crimes of the Reign of Terror of 1793–94 were providential punishments for a people beguiled and led astray by Enlightenment delusions.

Maistre's analyses of contemporary events are not only insightful but enduring. Despite the stupendous social, political, and technological developments of the past two centuries, his counsel remains relevant because human nature remains unchanged. To a fallen race, forbidden fruit remains the sweetest, in both private and public life. Though details differ, the transgressive principles he identified in the French Revolution continue to agitate societies to this day. Utopian aspiration—now hoary with age and burdened by a hundred failed experiments—continues vigorously to advance its hydra-headed agenda, ever hopeful of attaining its ever-receding goals. As it does so, it continues to provoke antipathy among those opposed to its dicta of theory and practice. Maistre was one such opponent, uniquely placed and abundantly gifted. To paraphrase A. N. Whitehead, philosophy is a series of footnotes to Plato. So, too, anti-revolutionary theory is a series of footnotes to Maistre. For it was he who first expounded the elements of a comprehensive criticism of revolutionary principles.

In the following chapters, we will examine Maistre's life and doctrine, the traditionalism and esotericism he shares with René Guénon, his enthusiasm for Freemasonry, his stature as a counter-Enlightenment figure, his ardent promotion of Roman Catholicism over Protestantism, his critique of America and its republican form of government, and his general relevance to the current religious and cultural scene.

Thus we proceed, with an overview of his life and teachings.

1

The Life and the Doctrine

Joseph de Maistre

WHENEVER the name of Joseph de Maistre is raised and recognized, it seems his crepuscular reputation has preceded him. It is not hard to understand why, for he had the ability to startle and even horrify his readers. Though a just and kind-hearted man by all accounts, he never blinded himself to unpalatable truths nor watered down their expression

His famous—or infamous—portrait of the public executioner, a discourse justifying the necessity of this disturbing agent of the state, is a notorious example. Make no mistake: he saw in the executioner an indispensable calling, filled by a peculiar man: a man foreign to the common run of humanity, inexplicable, extraordinary, a species unto himself. Though shunned by others, though set apart with his wife and offspring, he remained, in Maistre's view, essential to social order.

Let us listen to a passage from *Les Soirées de St. Pétersbourg* (*The Saint Petersburg Dialogues*): "A dismal signal is given; a minor judicial official comes to his [the executioner's] house to warn him that he is needed; he leaves; he arrives at some public place packed with a dense and throbbing crowd. A poisoner, a parricide, or a blasphemer is thrown to him; he seizes him, he stretches him on the ground, he ties him to a horizontal cross, he raises it up: then a dreadful silence falls, and nothing can be heard except the crack of bones...."[1]

---

1. *The Works of Joseph de Maistre*, selected, translated, and introduced by Jack Lively (New York: The Macmillan Company, 1965), 192. For those curious to read the rest of the passage, here it is: "...bones breaking under the crossbar and the

An appalling scene to be sure, especially in a day when many flinch from the very idea of capital punishment, even if performed by the injection of relatively painless chemicals into the veins of the most heinous of criminals. It is hardly surprising, then, that such a passage has marked Joseph de Maistre as a devotee of the morbid and macabre, and his foes have made the most of it. Nor do his writings on warfare, blood sacrifice, or the Spanish Inquisition do anything to dispel the stereotype. Beyond a doubt, he harbored a lifelong fascination with violence and irrationality. Beyond a doubt, he relished pushing principles to their logical conclusions and—it must be admitted—probably enjoyed shocking his readers from time to time. And yet, as we shall see, the author of such words was a man of personal and public decency, of great loyalty and probity, of kindness and generosity. At no time was he accused of being uncharitable or of intentionally harming anyone. Moreover, his works are characterized much less by such sanguinary passages than one might think, considering the notoriety attached to them.

Yet predictably, such passages have never failed to catch the eye of critics. No less a figure than Isaiah Berlin, the philosopher and historian of ideas, helped perpetuate the notion of Maistre as a proponent of—as opposed to a commentator on—violence and irra-

---

howls of the victim. He unfastens him; he carries him to a wheel: the shattered limbs interweave with the spokes; the head falls; the hair stands on end, and the mouth, open like a furnace, gives out spasmodically only a few blood-spattered words calling for death to come. He [the executioner] is finished: his heart flutters, but it is with joy; he congratulates himself, he says sincerely, *No one can break men on the wheel better than I.* He steps down; he stretches out his blood-stained hand, and justice throws into it from a distance a few pieces of gold which he carries through a double row of men drawing back with horror. He sits down to a meal and eats; then to bed, where he sleeps... Is this a man? Yes: God receives him in his temples and permits him to pray. He is not a criminal, yet it is impossible to say, for example, that he *is virtuous, that he is an honest man, that he is estimable,* and so on.... And yet all grandeur, all power, all subordination rests on the executioner: he is the horror and the bond of human association. Remove this incomprehensible agent from the world, and at that very moment order gives way to chaos, thrones topple, and society disappears. God, who is the author of sovereignty, is the author also of chastisement." Owing to his youthful membership in the *pénitents noirs,* Maistre may have personally witnessed such horrors, since the order encouraged its members to be present at executions to solace the condemned.

tionality, and to anachronistically view him as a precursor of fascist and other totalitarian systems. E. M. Cioran, the Romanian philosopher and essayist, took much the same view but from a different perspective, praising Maistre for the very things that Berlin condemned him. Disagreeing with received opinion, Cioran—a nihilist with a dubious political past—read Maistre approvingly as a man ahead of his time, as a proto-modernist whose calculated "monstrosity" and "odiousness" prefigured things to come.[2]

For dissimilar reasons, then, Cioran was no more likely than Berlin to draw favorable attention to Maistre's banner. Happily for our subject, others have taken a second look at the relevant facts. As a result, Maistre is receiving increasingly positive attention from mainstream scholars, who value his clear-eyed account of human nature and historical events in their many degrees of good and evil, virtue and vice.

One such scholar, Carolina Armenteros, has re-discovered the kinder and gentler Maistre, a man who for nearly forty years led a calm and uneventful life, first as a magistrate and then as a senator, prior to the invasion of his homeland by French armies in 1792. Driven into near-permanent exile, Maistre's ordeal stirred the depths of his soul and produced the brilliant thinker and writer he was to become. According to Armenteros, the conservative doctrine he then developed was not a "simplistic recrudescence of Old Regime ideology," changeless, reactionary, and reflexive, but instead the innovative link between Enlightenment philosophers of history and the traditionalist, socialist, and positivist philosophers that arose in his wake between 1820 and mid-century.[3] She maintains that Maistre's view of Providence, often criticized as little more than the agent of regenerative punishment, was of a knowledge that bestowed radical freedom by revealing its purposes to humanity. Hence it was a means of divine pedagogy, "the incarnation of the Enlightenment belief that human beings, no longer hopelessly

---

2. Owen Bradley, *A Modern Maistre: The Social & Political Thought of Joseph de Maistre* (Lincoln and London: University of Nebraska Press, 1999), xviii.

3. Carolina Armenteros, *The French Idea of History: Joseph de Maistre and His Heirs, 1794–1854* (Cornell University Press, Ithaca and London, 2011), 4.

embroiled in the toils of original sin, can be reformed and improved by knowledge."[4]

And so it goes: historians, philosophers, literary critics, and others have registered their yeas and nays over the years. Maistre has been weighed in the balance and found either wanting or worth a second look. Commentators have viewed him as a stylish misanthrope or as the noble defender of traditional morals and metaphysics. Let us take a look for ourselves, beginning at the beginning.

Maistre was born April 1, 1753, in the duchy of Savoy, in the capital of Chambéry. This Alpine province was French in language and culture but politically part of the northern Italian kingdom of Piedmont-Sardinia. Though Maistre would earn fame as a French author, he never lived in France and visited Paris only once, at the age of sixty-four.

Savoy's ties to Italy were of great importance to the Maistre family, for Joseph's father, François-Xavier Maistre, had come to Chambéry from Nice, which also belonged to Piedmont-Sardinia. Though Joseph believed his ancestors were of noble French blood, the most reliable evidence suggests a more humble origin, traceable to Nice as well. It appears the ancestral line included a mule driver who became a prosperous miller with property to his name, followed by an even more prosperous cloth merchant (Joseph's great-grandfather) who left a modest fortune to his descendants. Joseph's grandfather, André de Maistre, entered the lower ranks of the legal profession, received a rich dowry, and—despite setbacks during the French occupation of Nice in 1708–9—became a municipal official and adopted the coat of arms and motto that Joseph inherited (*Fors l'honneur nul souci*—"No care save honor"). It was left to Joseph's father, François-Xavier, to be incorporated into the nobility. Born in 1706, the elder Maistre held several legal posts before the king transferred him to the Senate of Savoy, wherein he served with distinction and rose to Second President of that body.

Young Joseph was groomed to follow in the paternal footsteps. Though no contemporary evidence is available, it is likely he was

---

4. Ibid., 2.

educated at least partly by Jesuits, who maintained a boarding school in Chambéry and directed religious confraternities there. It is also likely he attended the *collége royal* in Chambéry, which had been founded by Jesuits but was reorganized as a royal institution in 1729, with members of the order excluded from teaching.

Joseph was enrolled in the elite Jesuit confraternity, the *Congrégation Notre-Dame de l'Assomption*, as early as 1760, at the age of seven. This body, to which Joseph's father belonged, required an annual retreat and taught its members the *Spiritual Exercises* of St. Ignatius, with emphasis on daily examination of conscience. According to Richard Lebrun, dean of Maistre studies, the tenor of Jesuit teaching—despite past accusations of laxity—had become notable for a pessimistic view of the human race, based on the belief that original sin had all but vitiated human nature. Their instruction, then, later described and praised by Maistre, aimed at strict obedience, plenty of hard work, and protection from worldly corruption. A book of offices and prayers printed in 1768, Lebrun notes, carried an image of a "death's head" and a meditation "stressing the terrifying choice between penitence and damnation."[5]

It was a religion laden with guilt, punishment, and fear of God, hence at odds with an earlier and milder Jesuit piety. It appears the Savoyard spirituality of the time resonated to this sterner side of the faith, embodying as it did a near Jansenist rigorism,[6] not so much doctrinally as experientially. Though Maistre would become a vehement lifelong critic of Jansenism, it is no less true that the movement would indirectly influence his orthodoxy, as much as did the piety of the gentle St. Francis de Sales, whose teaching had greatly influenced his father.

---

5. Richard A. Lebrun, *Joseph de Maistre: An Intellectual Militant* (Kingston and Montreal: McGill-Queen's University Press, 1988), 14–15.

6. Jansenism was a Catholic movement based on the *Augustinus* of Cornelius Jansen (1585–1638). Doctrinally, it stressed predestination, man's moral inability, the absolute necessity of God's grace, and the irresistibility of that grace. The term "Jansenism" was coined by the Jesuits, who accused the movement of Calvinist affinities. Its most celebrated exponent was the mathematician, scientist, and religious writer Blaise Pascal. Innocent X condemned it as heretical in 1653.

The formal influence of Francis came to Joseph by way of the *pénitents noirs* (Black Penitents), into which he was initiated in 1768. Francis had co-founded the order in the late sixteenth century. Though its original focus had been on practical charity, it had become—like other confraternities of Joseph's time—preoccupied with mortality. Thus its iconography featured symbols of death in its chapel and devotional literature, and members wore black hoods in procession. The *memento mori* (reminder of death) and the *ars bene moriendi* (the art of dying well) were important features of the order.[7] It is unclear, however, to what extent Joseph assimilated these things, for he departed for university studies the year of his initiation.

Be that as it may, the religious ambience in which he was raised fashioned a man double in himself, a man combining in one person quite different and incompatible selves. No one could put it better than Maistre himself, when he wrote in 1795, in the second chapter of his essay, *"De l'état de Nature"* (*On the State of Nature*), the following: "Man is an enigma whose knot has never ceased to occupy observers. The contradictions he embodies astonishes reason and imposes silence on it. So what is this inconceivable being who carries within himself conflicting powers compelling him to self-hate for the sake of self-esteem?"[8] This divide would disquiet Maistre his entire life, causing endless introspection while stimulating the subtle awareness of a great writer.

Added to the influence of the *Congrégation Notre-Dame* and the *pénitents noir* was the example of Joseph's parents. Devout Catholics of great rectitude, they practiced an unwavering traditional piety. Madame Maistre expressed her faith by helping neighbors and assisting the sick and the poor, while François-Xavier followed the teaching of the above-mentioned Francis de Sales, with its "profound faith in providence, a confidence that God does what is best for our interests, and that He knows better than we do what we

7. Lebrun, *Joseph de Maistre*, 15.
8. Jean-Louis Darcel, "The Sources of Maistrian Sensibility," *Maistre Studies*, trans. and ed. Richard A. Lebrun (Lanham, MD, New York, London: University Press of America, 1988), 101.

need. This was a faith characterized by the humility of the sinner as well as stoic calm."[9] Joseph clearly absorbed this sense of God's providence, as his mature writings confirm time and again. His experience of confraternities played their role as well, especially in shaping his moral integrity and sense of duty, not to mention his darker visions and the inner divide with which he wrestled.

In the eyes of Joseph and his family, there was nothing theoretical about God's providence, for they believed it was evident during a serious illness that struck Joseph at the age of nine. According to his father, the boy's recovery was "graciously willed" by God, "by a particular grace... He had been reduced to the last extremities, he had received extreme unction, when by a happy revolution, we observed a diminution of the illness just when we thought he was going to expire."[10] As the family saw it, divine intervention saved the boy. No providentialist mind would ever be embarrassed by such a belief.

At sixteen (the year he entered the *pénitents*), Joseph was sent to the University of Turin for legal training. A gifted and hard-working student, he completed the program in three years, receiving his doctorate in April 1772. During that time, he was required to read Enlightenment authors, though earlier he had read Voltaire on his own. A budding *encyclopédist* himself, he compiled a personal dictionary of the arts and sciences, making use of his classical education and the newer learning. Seeking to reconcile the latest theories with his faith and earlier education, he concluded that belief in immortality was the only sanction for morality, even while jotting down "his first reflections on the happiness of criminals and virtuous men—the very debate that would open *Les soirées de Saint-Pétersbourg*... thirty-nine years later."[11]

On returning home from Turin, Maistre became a magistrate in Savoy's legal establishment. Hardly content to limit his mind to the demands of work, he spent two decades reading widely in history, philosophy, law, and theology, not to mention esoteric and occult material. He enlarged the already substantial library inherited from

9. Lebrun, *Joseph de Maistre*, 13.
10. Ibid., 14.
11. Armenteros, *The French Idea of History*, 22.

his maternal grandfather Demotz, turning it into the best library in Savoy. In the course of his studies, he became conversant in six modern European languages in addition to Latin and Greek.[12]

During this period he also embraced Freemasonry, which became a lifelong source of religious and philosophical reflection and—for much of the pre-Revolutionary period—a focal point of fashionable social life. With the outbreak of revolution in France, however, Freemasonry fell under suspicion and Maistre's lodge—at the request of King Victor Amadeus III—discontinued its meetings. Nonetheless, Maistre retained a vital interest in Masonry for the rest of his life, and it figures significantly in his writings.

That René Guénon, Maistre's twentieth century analogue, was involved in Freemasonry will provide fodder for exposition and comparison in chapter three. This is the case especially in that Freemasonry can be viewed—as Maistre and Guénon did view it—as a science of sacred symbols, in which correspondences between all parts of the universe, seen and unseen, may be discerned. This understanding is based on the notion of the universal interdependence of all things in both microcosm and macrocosm, a principle that commanded the unwavering assent of both men.

Maistre's steady and predictable public and private life in Savoy, enriched on the side by Masonic and scholarly pursuits, came to an end in 1792 when the Revolutionary armies of France crossed the frontier and occupied his homeland. A senator by this time as well as a magistrate, he was the only Savoyard of his rank to flee the homeland, taking his family with him to Aosta in northern Italy. Though ever loyal to his king, he was unsuccessful in obtaining a position at the royal court in Turin.

Two months after the family had fled to Italy, his wife re-crossed the Alps—without Joseph's knowledge—in an attempt to save the family's property from confiscation by the French authorities. Maistre returned to Chambéry himself but quickly found life intolerable under the new regime. Adding insult to injury, he was ordered to financially support French troops in their war against the Piedmontese army, in which his own brothers were serving. Hence

12. Ibid., 23.

the family fled again, leaving its property behind, including most of Joseph's library.

For the next four years, the Maistres lived in cramped rented quarters among the émigré community in Lausanne, and for the following twenty-five Joseph remained in exile, with most of that time spent as ambassador to Russia in the service of his king, Victor Emmanuel I. He found himself not only physically exiled from the world he had known since birth but spiritually and philosophically exiled also, profoundly alienated from the currents of thought and practice that had first convulsed France, then swept through his homeland and engulfed ever larger parts of Europe.

Yet for all its drawbacks, the period in Lausanne was the incubator of a great and powerful writer. Stung into militant anti-revolutionary consciousness, and no doubt inspired by conversations in the salons of the French woman of letters Madame de Staël and others, he learned to fight fire with fire. No longer content to write occasional compositions of an edifying and moralistic nature, he turned his vast erudition into a polemical arsenal aimed at the Revolution and the *philosophes* whose writings had paved the way for the republican triumph. Taking a page from Voltaire, he cultivated the irony, invective, and derision of the Revolutionary spirit so characteristic of his foes and turned it against them. Thus Maistre the pamphleteer was born. His newfound vocation found its voice in the classic *Considérations sur la France* in 1797, the work that established his reputation as a master of polemic and a thinker not to be trifled with.

Also in 1797, Maistre's king made peace with Napoléon by ceding Savoy and Nice to France. At the same time, Maistre was momentarily recalled to Turin but the advance of French armies soon had him on the run again. The family arrived in Venice in mid-winter and subsisted by selling silver plate that Mme. Maistre had brought from Savoy. The family's fortunes at last took a turn for the better in late 1799 when Joseph was asked to serve as Regent of Sardinia, the highest judicial post on the island. Though the appointment relieved the family's financial difficulties, and though he performed his duties humanely and professionally, native Sardinians were unhappy to have a Savoyard exercising authority over them. Moreover, Charles-Felix the Viceroy was at odds with Maistre over how best to discipline the unruly islanders, with the former intent on employing a harsh, military form of justice while Maistre insisted on correct civil procedures. A personality conflict also appears to have come into play, and Charles-Felix asked the king for Maistre's recall.

The conflict was resolved when the king appointed Maistre to serve as ambassador to Russia. This might seem a welcome development given the strained relations on Sardinia, but Maistre was distressed at the thought of family separation. Owing to a change in relations between France and Piedmont, he had already sent his wife, son, and eldest daughter back to northern Italy, where his children could get a proper education. But now... to Russia? Ever dutiful, he accepted the appointment and thus began a fifteen-year absence—1803 to 1817—from not only his homeland but from Western Europe itself.

When finally joined by his family in 1814, Maistre considered spending the rest of his days in Russia. For he had—despite the long and lonely years as the impoverished ambassador of a frequently ungrateful king—enjoyed several personal triumphs. As a man of integrity and unswerving loyalty to his monarch, he had early gained the respect of the diplomatic community. Moreover, his charm and wit made him a popular figure in the salons, and Tsar Alexander I was far from immune to the Savoyard's magnetism. Thus Maistre's influence was far greater than one might expect from the ambassador of so minor a kingdom, and his achievements were personal as well as public. Through his good offices, his brother, Xavier, was given a high post in the Russian civil service; his son, Rudolphe, became an officer in the Russian Royal Guard, and the Jesuit order received a charter for its college in Potolsk. Above all, he kept his pen busy writing memoirs on education, science, religion and illuminism for his Russian ministerial friends, alongside more substantial works such as *Les Soirées de Saint-Pétersbourg* and *L'Examen de la Philosophie de Bacon* (*An Examination of the Philosophy of Bacon*), both published posthumously, and *Du Pape* (*On the Pope*) and *De l'église gallicane* (*The Gallican Church*), both published after he left Russia. Privately, he circulated his work

The Life and the Doctrine

on political constitutions, *Essai sur le Principe générateur des Constitutions Politiques* (*Essay on the Generative Principle of Political Constitutions*), to thwart the plans of the Russian reformer Michael Speranski.[13]

Owing to Orthodox enmity, the Jesuits were eventually banished from the capital and, by action of Czar Alexander, Maistre along with them. Having been accused of making converts among the upper classes, and thus in disfavor, Maistre sought permission to be recalled and Victor-Emmanuel I granted the request. Thus the Maistre family left Russia in the summer of 1817. Alexander, who remained on friendly terms with Maistre, arranged for the ambassador's family to return to Le Havre on a Russian naval vessel. It was on this journey that Maistre made his only visit to Paris.

Returning to Piedmont, Maistre spent the last four years of his life in Turin. Although given an important-sounding but mostly honorary position in the government, he found plenty of time to edit the works he had written while abroad. Presciently and sadly, he seems to have "sensed the strength and ultimate triumph of the forces he had always opposed."[14] That realization, coupled with dissatisfaction with the Restoration in France he had so long desired, cast a melancholy shadow over his last years, despite the presence of his beloved family. Convinced the old Europe was dead and gone, he died in February 1821 at the age of sixty-seven.

René Guénon

As indicated, René Guénon[15] will serve as our link between traditionalist thought as it was pioneered by Joseph de Maistre something over two-hundred years ago and as it was taken up by Guénon and his followers in the twentieth century. As mentioned, the sur-

13. Richard A. Lebrun, *Throne and Altar: The Political and Religious Thought of Joseph de Maistre* (Ottawa, Canada: University of Ottawa Press, 1965), 13.
14. Ibid., 14.
15. The following summary of René Guénon's life and thought has been culled from various standard sources, but in particular from the writings of traditionalists Harry Oldmeadow and Jean Borella, along with Guénon's friend, publisher, and first biographer, Paul Chacornac.

prising similarities between these authors in biography and literary content are several in number.

In the following chapters, Guénon will be something of a secondary figure, inasmuch as Maistre is the main focus of our work. Nonetheless, Guénon remains a significant figure in certain conservative circles, owing to his role as providential interpreter of tradition and as founder of the traditionalist or perennialist school in the twentieth century. Hence a summary of his life and work is not out of place here, as an introduction for those new to him (and to the authors who have continued his work) and as a refresher for those familiar with him. Admittedly, he is not widely known, but then how many metaphysicians and other serious writers are household names? Those with ears to hear are drawn to his voice and edified when they hear it.

The future metaphysician and author was born in 1886 in the historic city of Blois, along the banks of the Loire in north-central France. The only son of an architect, the fragile boy lived a sheltered life in his early years. Mme. Duru, his maternal aunt and a next-door neighbor, grew attached to him and spoiled him like a mother. A primary school teacher in Blois, she taught him the rudiments of learning.

Like Joseph de Maistre, Guénon grew up in a conservative Catholic milieu and, when formal schooling began, was educated by Jesuits. A brilliant student, he often ranked first in his class. He attended Notre Dame des Aydes from 1898 to 1901, at which time a quarrel with a teacher resulted in withdrawal from the school. In January 1902, he entered the College Augustin-Thierry, where again he was an outstanding student, excelling in philosophy and sciences. He obtained the first part of his *Baccalauréat* in August of the same year and completed it in philosophy in July 1903, but with the disappointing citation of "satisfactory." Enrolled in the mathematics program in 1904, he demonstrated great aptitude and earned the college's highest award, a medal offered by the Alumni Association. In addition, his philosophy professor stated that he was an "excellent student."

Encouraged by his teachers, he applied to Rollin College in Paris and was accepted as a candidate in advanced mathematics, beginning in October 1904. Before long, he found the boisterous life of the Latin Quarter irksome, and had difficulty in keeping up with his studies. Finding little changed in his second year, he abandoned both his studies and the Latin Quarter for the peace of the Ile Saint-Louis, where he was to live for most of the next quarter century.

At the end of 1906, he began a journey through the underworld of French occultism. Soon he became a leading member of theosophical, spiritualist, Masonic (an important link with Maistre), and neo-gnostic societies. In June 1909, he founded the occultist journal *La Gnose*, which lasted over two years and served as the vehicle for most of his early writings. He may also have received Taoist or Islamic initiations in this period, and he made important contacts with members of the Advaita school of Vedanta, whose instruction grounded him in Hindu metaphysics in ways that academic orientalism could not match.

The year 1912 marked Guénon's break with occultist affiliations and, on a personal note, his marriage to Berthe Loury, an assistant to his aunt and childhood teacher, Mme. Duru. The Guénons soon welcomed Mme. Duru and a four-year-old niece, Françoise, into their household. Dwelling "in the midst of this triple feminine affection,"[16] Guénon needed to earn a living for himself and his dependents, his private means having dwindled. Exempt for health reasons from military service in World War One, he earned a bachelor's degree of arts from the Sorbonne in 1915, followed by his *maîtrise* with a thesis on Leibniz's infinitesimal calculus. Henceforth he was qualified to teach philosophy, which he did in various Catholic boarding schools from 1915–1929, with the exception of a professorship for a year in Sétif, Algeria, overlapping 1917–18. There he suffered a burdensome teaching load, not only in philosophy but also in French and Latin. Having learned the rudiments of Arabic earlier, it is believed he perfected his knowledge of that language while in Algeria. It was also the first time he was exposed to prolonged

---

16. Jean Borella, "René Guénon and the Traditionalist School," *Modern Esoteric Spirituality*, ed. Antoine Faivre and Jacob Needleman, vol. 21, *World Spirituality* (New York: The Crossroad Publishing Company, 1995), 333.

contact with Islam, and he may have made contacts with traditional Muslim leaders.

After having emerged from the secretive world of Parisian occultism, he had begun moving in intellectual and social circles in an intensely Catholic milieu. He was influenced by such prominent Catholic intellectuals as Jacques Maritain, Fathers Émile Peillaube and Antonin-Gilbert Sertillanges, and one M. Milhaud, who taught on the philosophy of science at the Sorbonne. The years 1912 to 1930 were the most public of Guénon's life, during which he attended lectures at the Sorbonne (lecturing once himself) and wrote and published widely. His first books appeared in the 1920s, gaining for him a reputation for his treatment of philosophical and metaphysical subjects.

During this period, Guénon also explored the possibility of recovering esoteric traditions within Catholicism, thus reviving the exoteric faith by exploration of interior doctrines and practices. He contributed regularly to the Catholic journal *Regnabit*, the Sacre-Coeur review founded and edited by Father Jean-Émile Anizan. "Traditional" Christian perspectives became a central theme in his articles, of which five appear in a later collection (*Fundamental Symbols: The Universal Language of Sacred Science*).

The years 1927–1930 witnessed major changes in Guénon's life. A conflict between Anizan (whom Guénon supported) and the Archbishop of Reims, as well as adverse criticism of his book, *The King of the World* (1927), brought matters to a head regarding Guénon's suspicion that the Catholic Church had surrendered to temporal and material concerns. Moreover, Guénon's wife died unexpectedly during a surgical procedure, and within a year Mme. Duru also died. Six months later his niece returned to live with her mother and Guénon found himself alone.

In September 1929, he met Marie Dina, the widow of an Egyptian engineer and daughter of a Canadian railway baron. An admirer of his work, she offered to create a publishing house to bring out his books along with translations he was to make of Sufi texts. In order to find the latter, they left for Cairo in March 1930. After three months, and in need of more time to finish his task, Guénon remained in Cairo while Mme. Dina returned to France, where she abandoned the project. For the next two years, Guénon lived in poverty, even as he immersed himself in Arabic culture and the Muslim religion. Eventually, his life stabilized and he chose to stay in Egypt, where he now spoke Arabic without an accent. He frequented El-Azhar University, wrote articles for an Egyptian review, continued to publish books, and was initiated into the Sufi order of Shadhilites with the name of Abdel Wahed Yahya. In 1934 he married Fatima, the eldest daughter of an Egyptian friend, Sheikh Muhammad Ibrahim. The couple had two daughters and two sons, the younger of the sons born after Guénon's death in 1951.

Guénon's books and articles may be divided into six categories: the early occult writings, metaphysics, criticism of the modern world, tradition, symbolism, and spiritual realization. Although his doubts about occultist groups were growing in the 1909–12 period, he only critiqued them fully with the appearance of *Theosophy: History of a Pseudo-Religion* (1921) and *The Spiritist Fallacy* (1923), the lengthiest books he was to write. As used in the title of the first-mentioned book, "theosophy" referred to Madame Blavatsky's Theosophical Society, a movement founded in the last quarter of the nineteenth century. The movement's doctrines were drawn from a range of sources, including the authentic theosophical tradition, various additional esoteric teachings and figures, and an admixture of original and—in Guénon's decided view—dubious contemporary material.

Guénon's interest in Eastern traditions, which characterized his writings for the rest of his life, had been awakened around 1909, as intimated above, and some of his early articles in *La Gnose* were devoted to Vedantic metaphysics. His first book, *Introduction to the Study of the Hindu Doctrines* (1921), has received much praise over the years for its understanding of its subject but it earned no plaudits from the academic establishment of its day. When Guénon presented it to the Sorbonne as a doctoral thesis, it was rejected by the orientalist and indologist Sylvain Lévi. Although Guénon suspected a conspiracy was afoot, it is fair to note that Lévi applied normal research requirements to the thesis, and in these Guénon was clearly deficient, despite the merits of the work otherwise.

Guénon's principal treatment of Hinduism, *Man and his Becom-*

ing According to the Vedanta, was published in 1925. Other significant works on Eastern subjects included *Oriental Metaphysics*,
delivered as a lecture at the Sorbonne in 1925 but not published
until 1939; *The Great Triad*, based on Taoist doctrine, and articles on
Hindu mythology, Taoism, Confucianism, and reincarnation (a
concept Guénon dismissed).

Despite his interest in the East, Guénon did not neglect the West.
While moving in Catholic circles in the 1920s, he explored various
aspects of Europe's spiritual heritage, with articles on the Druids,
the Grail, Christian symbolism, and folkloric motifs. He also wrote
several longer works, among them *The Esoterism of Dante* (1925), *St.
Bernard* (1929), *The Symbolism of the Cross* (1931), and *Spiritual
Authority and Temporal Power* (1929). Although such writings are
erudite and compelling, Jean Borella, a traditionalist himself, suggests that "a profound comprehension of the Christian 'form' always
escaped Guénon." He was, Borella allows, "certainly capable of
explaining elements of the Christian faith such as scriptural or litur-
gical symbols, and he offered remarkable, sometimes definitive,
interpretations; but he was not in a position to accept the paradox
of a religion that . . . ignores the institutional distinction of esoterism and exoterism and whose function is to proclaim the greatest
mysteries in the public place."[17]

Two other books, which tie together certain of his central themes,
are his masterpiece, *The Reign of Quantity and the Signs of the Times*
(1945) and the earlier *The Crisis of the Modern World* (1927). Their
subject matter had appeared even earlier with *East and West* (1924).
In the *Reign of Quantity*, an increasingly pessimistic Guénon not
only attacked modernity but discerned a "counter-tradition" at
work, in which inverted spiritualities were penetrating the cracks of
a solidified, materialistic society and reintroducing dark forces from
"below."

Such in overview is the life and doctrine of René Guénon.
Though his influence remains negligible in Western academia, he
casts a spell on those drawn to him and to his powerful and timeless
message. To cite Jean Borella once again: "[N]o one can read

17. Ibid., 336.

Guénon without experiencing the quite extraordinary feeling that all which human reason had more or less obscurely dreamed, all that the great sages in times past had taught but which seemed lost, all that glistened in the deceiving forms of a multiple occult tradition—all this finally finds an order and becomes possibly true. From this point of view, the work produced a kind of 'miracle,' it breaks down the fundamental incredulity of modern readers; it awakens in them a forgotten intelligence."[18]

It is an achievement likely to gain in recognition in years to come. The more time passes, the more Guénon's message discovers to attentive readers the perennial truth on which a life can be founded. It is indeed, in these days of dissolution, something of a "miracle."

18. Ibid.

2
Theosophy and
Its Compensations

BENEATH his austere Catholicism, there ran in Joseph de Maistre a teeming current of theosophical speculation and conviction. Part complement and part compensation, it invoked his Muse, nourished his imagination, and deepened his insights.

It answered also the need for unification in a man double in himself. On one side was a self-abasing sinner and dutiful burdened citizen; on the other, an illuminated adept and cosmopolitan litterateur. Traits of saint and sinner contended within him, and an unsparing conscience detected the least infraction. How might one resolve this disharmony?

Theosophy—esotericism generally, for that matter—is a perennial means of addressing just such concerns, of achieving "the union of opposites," of equilibrating the soul. The attraction for Maistre is not hard to see. Much theosophical benefit came to him (as it did to René Guénon) by way of Freemasonry, which will be examined in the next chapter, but other sources were equally in play.

As noted earlier, both theosophy and "perennial philosophy"[1] provided the foundation from which Maistre's esoteric thought emerged. Dismissing the lure of the *philosophes*, he anchored himself in the ancient and early modern luminaries of a prior mode of

---

1. As indicated in notes two and three in the "Introduction," we use "theosophy"—an integrated knowledge of the relations between God, humanity, and the universe—as more or less an umbrella term for Maistre's esoteric expressions, which sought a unitive vision of the various levels of reality. The writings of Louis-Claude de Saint-Martin (1743–1803), a theosopher of the purest strain, were a significant influence on Maistre. "Perennial philosophy" maintains that the world's religious traditions are based on variations of the one primordial tradition.

reflection. Members of this line included Pythagoras and Plato; Cicero, Origen, and Augustine; René Descartes, Ralph Cudworth, and Bishop Bossuet; Leibnitz, Nicolas Malebranche, and Archbishop Fénelon. "I shall not give the names of the spokesmen for the other side," Maistre declared, "for they offend my tongue. When I am ignorant about a problem, I decide without any reason other than my taste for good company and my aversion for bad."[2]

It is likely that exile from his homeland only heightened Maistre's interest in theosophical speculation and practice. The interest was hardly new to him, for Freemasonry had stimulated and cultivated a form of it for nearly two decades. But when Masonic practice was no longer readily available, he turned to additional sources, as we shall see below.

In all of this, one could say Maistre was something of a double exile, physically separated from Savoy and metaphorically separated within himself. But this raises the question: whence the inner separation, the sharp dichotomies, in so accomplished a man? Clearly they were rooted in his early years, as such things almost always are. In large part, they derived from nothing more complicated than the "human condition," which has pitted man—especially introspective man—against himself from the beginning. Yet in Maistre, awareness of the divide appears to have been more pronounced than in most others. As nurture worked on nature, the discipline of the Jesuits and the religious confraternities surely had a hand in deepening it, as did the high standards and expectations of his devoted family and the conservative milieu of Savoy itself. Such influences were the civilizing forces of his life, imparted with the best of intentions, yet perhaps overly strict for a youth of sensitive nature.

The sense of inner exile was acute during Maistre's years in Lausanne, where he and his family lived among émigrés in the midst of a foreign population. Epitome of classical rigor and orthodox belief he remained, yet a displaced soul, robbed of stability in time and place, he had become, with no relief in sight. He compensated by becoming something of a pre-Romantic: an artist and thinker

2. *The Saint Petersburg Dialogues*, in *The Works of Joseph de Maistre*, trans. Jack Lively, 207.

increasingly open to the intuitive and the irrational. His agitated soul required more than ever the warm streams of esotericism to assuage the rigor of his inherited orthodoxy. In the years ahead, this denizen of the émigré communities of southern Europe and the diplomatic salons of St. Petersburg would become ever more observant of the "universal discord we call life"[3] in both the inner and outer worlds, his own prominently included.

Though longing for his homeland and ill at ease in his straightened circumstances, Maistre was solaced in Lausanne by a surprising number of kindred souls, for Switzerland had long been a home for esoterically-minded thinkers. In 1774, Jean-Philippe Dutoit-Membrini, a native of Moudon in the Vaud canton, had, by his writings and his animating presence, turned Lausanne into a center of theosophic activity. Others who added to the regional ambience included Niklaus Anton Kirchberger of Bern, a correspondent of Louis-Claude de Saint-Martin (of which more later); Karl von Eckartshausen, a prolific Bavarian writer on mysticism and alchemy; Johann Heinrich Jung-Stilling, a physician, professor at Marburg, and propagator of Jacob Böhme's teachings; and Johann Caspar Lavater, a Protestant clergyman and founder of physiognomy. Lavater, from Zurich, stressed the magical power of prayer, practiced magnetism, and demonstrated interest in theurgy. Another figure of note was Saint-Georges de Marsais, a frequent visitor to Switzerland and spiritual director of a community in Vaudois. He was an avid reader of the Quietists Antoinette Bourignon, François Fénelon, and Madame Guyon. Among such as these, or their persisting influence, the Savoyard exile found congenial company.

In Maistre's *Carnets* (notebooks), kept during the sojourn in Switzerland, we find a handful of enigmatic entries that provide clues to possible esoteric activities. In the words of Jean Rebotton, it seems that Maistre "lived a triple experience: that of astrological divination, that of theurgy, and that, finally, which involved a more interior mysticism purified of all magic practice."[4] As to the latter, Maistre was greatly influenced by Madame Guyon and Teresa of

3. Owen Bradley, *A Modern Maistre*, 5, 38.
4. Jean Rebotton, "Joseph a Floribus," in *Maistre Studies*, 155–56.

Avila, proponents of a transforming ascent through successive degrees of spiritual realization—of a contemplative exercise that liberated the human spirit from terrestrial forces. In the *Soirées*, written a couple of decades later, the "Senator" would echo Madame Guyon in this vein: "Sometimes I should like to spring beyond the narrow limits of this world, I should like to anticipate the day of revelations, and plunge myself into infinity."[5]

But what of the hints of theurgic and astrological practice? René Johannet, whose researches from 1932 are cited by Rebotton, wrote the following: "On three occasions during [Maistre's] stay in Lausanne, which was decisive for the growth of his ideas, we find . . . entries that, at first glance, seem incomprehensible." Made on Oct. 13, 1793, June 27, 1794, and July 2, 1795, the entries speak of a "georgic star," an entity causing melancholy. "Many times," Johannet continued, "Maistre spoke to his correspondents of the '*étoile des Maistre*,' a forbidding star that took happiness away." In light of this, he asked: "[A]re these entries not sufficiently clear? Must they not become convincing when it is recalled that at this time . . . Maistre had just bought Lalande's *Traite d'Astronomie*?"[6]

Rebotton finds the idea seductive but unpersuasive. He doubts that it was Maistre's private destiny that was in question. "To translate 'Georgium sydus' as 'georgic star' [*astre géorgique*]," he says, "does not seem very rigorous; Johannet confuses 'Georgium' and 'georgicum.'" Was it not in fact, he asks, "George's star" that was in question; the personage of George III, king of England? Indeed, at the time of the entry, Maistre had cast a longing eye on Britain, arch-enemy of the Revolution, as a possible ally. In February 1794, prior to the second entry in the *Carnets*, he did in fact cultivate close ties with John Trevor, British ambassador to Turin, and his wife. "Was he not asking if the salvation of Europe, and therefore his own, might not come from this monarch?"[7] There are more ques-

---

5. *St. Petersburg Dialogues: Or Conversations on the Temporal Government of Providence*, trans. and ed. Richard A. Lebrun (Montreal and Kingston: McGill-Queen's University Press, 1993), 293.

6. Rebotton, 156.

7. Ibid., 157.

tions than answers, it seems, though the first suggestion is a far more romantic one than the rather pedestrian second, and a better fit with the overall tenor of Maistre's esotericism, no matter how linguistically correct the second suggestion appears to be.

Rebotton also investigated the mysterious crosses and strange entries which appeared in the *Carnets* on suggestive dates in 1792. Could they refer to theurgic operations, that is, to ritual practices to invoke a deity? Having piqued our interest once again, Rebotton backs away from a decisive verdict, suggesting that theurgy was likely not in play. Such operations, he observes, were the special privilege of the Elus Cohens (*Elus Cöens* or "Elect Priests") and were rarely practiced within the Reformed Scottish rite in which Maistre had been active. In addition, the name of Maistre "nowhere figures on lists of the 'Elus.'" This being said, theurgy is not totally dismissed. For in 1792, Rebotton says, Maistre was in contact with fellow Masons Sebastien Giraud and Marc Revoire, both Cohens themselves. Could not one of them have initiated him? "Moreover," he continues, "it is known that the Elus Cohens officiated, by preference though not exclusively, during the three days following the equinox." Intriguingly, in 1792, the equinox fell precisely on one of the days marked by a cross in the *Carnets*, a day that was neither a religious feast nor a communion. In sum, Rebotton concludes, Maistre might have witnessed such operations though not practiced them himself.[8]

There is a third group of entries in the *Carnets* that is equally puzzling. The dates are March 10 and April 17, 1794, and March 10, 1795. They speak of a "metamorphosis." Rebotton "risks an interpretation," conjecturing that Maistre might have been seeking to "bilocate" himself—a truly exotic proposal. But might he not instead have been engaged in a contemplative exercise only, seeking by pure effort of soul to achieve "a kind of metamorphosis" that would liberate his spirit from terrestrial forces—a rather exotic feat itself? This notion brings to mind the influence of Madame Guyon, cited above. Again, the evidence is inconclusive.[9]

8. Ibid., 158–59.
9. Ibid., 159–60.

Each of the above entries was made during Maistre's years of greatest worldly misfortune, roughly 1792–99. In that period, his homeland had been overrun, his values overthrown, and his family cast into poverty and exile. Yet, from such misfortunes, a renewed and tempered Maistre began to emerge. During these years, he rediscovered a place of inner balance amidst the physical and emotional turmoil of revolution and exile, a measure of peace and intellectual coherence that reinvigorated his lifelong belief in Providence. He found at last a means of placing the Revolution in perspective, of seeing it under the aspect of God's eternal purposes. He thereby defused its power to agitate his soul, at least in part.

His new perspective makes an appearance in the *Discours à la marquise Costa de Beauregard* of 1794. "For a long time," he wrote in that work, "we have not understood the Revolution that we are witnessing. For a long time we have taken it for an *occurrence*. We were in error; this is an epoch; and unhappy are generations that assist at epochs of the world!" Unhappy they may be; but to persons of esoteric insight able to penetrate the veil of worldly incident and episode, a deeper understanding was possible. The flood of events that swept away the old order was, in Maistre's words, under governance of "the very good and very great Being." World historic events had unfolded according to pattern and purpose. "All the evils of which we are witnesses and victims," Maistre wrote, "can only be acts of justice or equally necessary means of regeneration."[10]

It was an *epoch* indeed, a distinctive period marked by features and events without precedent, with consequences felt in every country and in every domain of thought and action. The French Revolution was no mere rebellion against authority. It was instead the herald of an entirely new era, a unique age that would urge succeeding generations to attempt further novel experiments on the social fabric. Yet Maistre, grounded in newfound illumination, found a measure of optimism in the face of upheaval, convinced as he was that Providence was working its will in all manner of mysterious and condign ways.

10. Ibid., 161–62.

Maistre's new perspective on the Revolution and God's guiding hand in it bore fruit in his *Considerations on France* of 1797. Gestating for some time, it was inspired in part by the reading of Jean-Claude de Saint-Martin's *Lettre à un ami sur la Révolution francaise* (*Letter to a Friend on the French Revolution*), which had appeared in 1795. To be sure, Maistre had been under Saint-Martin's spell for several years, as noted above, having read *L'homme de désir* (*The Man of Desire*) shortly after it came from the presses in 1790 and other of his works in prior years.

In their respective interpretations, Saint-Martin and Maistre agreed on the supernatural character of the Revolution. They further agreed it had been God's intention to cleanse France of religious and political sin and to initiate an order of things more attuned to the divine plan. In holding that God's intervention was necessary, they believed men in their own strength and intelligence were too small and too weak to have accomplished the purposes they had intended. In support of this view, they pointed to the extraordinary power of the Revolution, so out of proportion—in their minds—to the mediocre personalities of its fomenters. How could these men, they asked, feckless in so many ways, have achieved unassisted the events that had deposed a king and turned a society upside down?

In Saint-Martin's view, divine involvement favored the Revolutionary cause in its cleansing of iniquity. Maistre by contrast maintained the decadent players of the *ancien régime* and the leaders of the Revolution were equally guilty, and that divine favor rested on neither. Yet he blamed the latter for the more heinous crime: an attack on established sovereignty. In all of this, he believed God was the director of events but not the author of evil. He it was who allowed the forces of destruction a free hand, to perform their refining work, but he was not their agent. Royalists and revolutionaries alike—indirect and unwitting instruments of the divine will—did the actual work themselves, sharing the stage and playing their parts.

During this time, Maistre drew inspiration from others besides Saint-Martin, and his interests ranged beyond the Revolution and its effects. More narrowly esoteric subjects continued to command his attention. Writers he sampled included William Law, the eighteenth century English disciple of Jacob Böhme, whose *The Spirit of Prayer* he read in 1796. In this work, Maistre encountered Law at his theosophical best, who in dialogue form treated fallen humanity, grace, conversion, regeneration, genuine devotion, and other subjects guaranteed to pique the interest of the religious soul. But it was one thing to read Law, whose rigor and common sense made even of Böhme a more or less comprehensible writer; it was quite another to be influenced by the German mystic himself. Although Böhme drew accolades from Law and Saint-Martin, Maistre gave him a cooler reception, calling him a "fanatic" in the *Soirées*. French clarity and vocabulary had met German opacity and imprecision, and they were not a match.

In addition to revolutionary ponderings, Maistre delved into pagan and Christian antiquity in search of buttressing illuminist and other theses. In 1797, he turned to Origen of Alexandria (AD 185?–254?), especially his ideas on redemption by blood, a Biblical motif that dovetailed with Maistre's thinking on the course of the Revolution, social order, and cosmology. According to Origen, the blood shed on Calvary "had been useful not only to Man, but to the angels, to the stars, to all created beings."[11] Maistre shared Origen's belief that the planets were "alive," part of a cosmos "created *by* and *for* intelligence."[12] Imbued with such notions, Maistre went so far as to urge the Platonic idea that the stars themselves were divinities, and to hold that at least some early Christians found this belief conformable to dogma and of use in their initiations.

The possibility that intelligent beings (aside from traditionally recognized entities, such as angels) in one form or another exist beyond the confines of earth was held also by René Guénon, although in somewhat different form. According to Guénon, tradition admits not only "the plurality of inhabited worlds, but also the plurality of humanities filling these worlds."[13] It is a view more con-

11. Antoine Faivre, *Theosophy, Imagination, Tradition: Studies in Western Esotericism* (Albany: State University of New York Press, 2000), 92.

12. Owen Bradley, *A Modern Maistre*, 157.

13. René Guénon, *Studies in Freemasonry & the Compagnonnage* (San Rafael, CA: Sophia Perennis, 2004), n. 12, 7.

genial to science, or at least to science fiction, than anything the pre-modern world might have contemplated, but that Guénon entertained it lends it a certain cachet.

Also under the influence of Alexandrian Christianity, Maistre ascribed souls to plants and animals as well as to planets, and blamed man's response to nature for having occasioned the Fall. Furthermore, he was influenced by Origen's teacher, Clement, who taught him lessons on allegory and priesthood from within the context of a "Hellenistic synthesis of Greek, Egyptian, and Judaic discourses."[14] Finally, the Alexandrians convinced him the soul was the mediating entity between spirit and body, a notion long held by esotericists and useful in addressing the dividedness and discord that occurs within a person. Maistre resonated with all of these speculations.

Contrary to the spirit of the age, and in line with esotericist thought in the main, Maistre looked for the reunion of science and religion. In the *Soirées*, he struck a prophetic note: "Would you like another proof of what is being prepared? Look for it in the sciences... But wait until the natural affinity of religion and science are brought together in the head of a single man of genius." In the wake of such a man, Maistre predicted the demise of profane science. "Then opinions that seem bizarre or nonsensical to us today will be axioms impossible to doubt. Then men will talk of our present *stupidity* as we talk of the superstition of the Middle ages." At the moment, Maistre proclaimed, European thinkers were like "conjurors or initiates" who had made a monopoly of science as they understood it in their own narrow and one-sided way, and who would not "have anyone know *more* or *other* than themselves." But truly enlightened men—unlike the *philosophes*—would make science appear in a far different light. At such a time, the human spirit would attain to its former exalted position. "It will be shown," Maistre said, "that all the ancient traditions are true, that all of paganism is nothing but a system of corrupted and displaced truths, which only need cleaning, so to speak, and restoring to their plane,

14. Bradley, *A Modern Maistre*, 107.

to shine forth all their light."[15] The ideas underpinning the materialism of the eighteenth and nineteenth centuries would be swept away. Restoration would occur. Deep and abiding traditions, traditions that had supported from time immemorial an exiled race in all its pathos and glory, would once again find their place in the sun.

Finally, in the *Soirées* and other writings, we find Maistre pondering not only the unity of science and religion but the unity of the self, of the interior being, that was so often on his mind and yet so elusive of realization. In notebook entries, he reflected theosophically on this theme by way of Plato's double man in the *Symposium*: "When life or exterior generation will have become similar to interior or angelic life, there will be but one birth. There will be no more gender. The male and the female will make but one and the realm of God will arrive." In support of this curious doctrine, calling to mind as it does the spiritual androgyny of esotericist speculation, Maistre draws on the apocryphal Jesus as reported by Clement, "the contemporary of the Apostles" (not to be confused with Clement of Alexandria). In the words of Clement's Jesus, the Kingdom will arrive "when two things become one, when what is outside resembles what is inside, when the Male is confounded with the Female, and there is neither man nor woman."[16] A related notion can be found in the canonical words of St. Luke, where Christ speaks of "those who are considered worthy of taking part . . . in the resurrection from the dead," of those who "will neither marry nor be given in marriage," of those who "can no longer die, for they are like the angels" (Luke 20:35–36). Drawn from classical, apocryphal, and canonical sources, the foregoing suggest an ultimate—albeit a seemingly eccentric—cure for the disequilibrium of human existence.

With varying degrees of success, Maistre sought to find just such a cure all his days.

15. *St. Petersburg Dialogues*, Lebrun, 325–26.
16. Bradley, *A Modern Maistre*, 174–75.

3

Maistre Among the Masons

JOSEPH DE MAISTRE and René Guénon both found in Freemasonry an unlikely supplement to their traditional and orthodox beliefs. Raised in conservative Catholic families, they yet resonated with the doctrine and symbolism of the Masonic lodge and its message of perennial wisdom. Despite reservations, they maintained an emotional attachment to Masonry throughout their lives.

Maistre became a Freemason in 1773, at the age of twenty, by joining the Trois Mortier lodge in Chambéry, a standard "blue lodge" connected to the Grand Orient of London. Though in doing so he followed the fashion of the day, one is justified in supposing a deeper motive. Judging from his seriousness as a member of confraternities; from his subsequent career in Masonry and interest in Masonic reform, and from his esotericist pursuits in general, it is clear his interest in Masonry was grounded in something more than fashionable behavior. It seems it was based on a felt need for the compensating balance of which we have already spoken, on a need to widen the bounds of a much-loved but rigorously one-sided Catholicism by way of complementary and expansive influences.

While active in Trois Mortier in Chambéry, Maistre and other members of the lodge developed an avid interest in the reform Masonry of Jean-Baptiste Willermoz, a cloth merchant in Lyon. Willermoz, it appears, taught a theurgy of magical rituals formulated to communicate with, and receive aid from, beneficent supernatural beings, a practice guaranteed to fire the imagination of aspiring adepts. When in 1776 he learned of the zeal for his system present in the Trois Mortier lodge, he awarded the grade of Chevalier Bienfaissant de la Cite Sainte (CBCS) to Maistre and two other Brothers, at which time Maistre took the name Joseph a Floribus. Later that year, Willermoz selected seven Brothers to be "the chiefs

35

and the founders of the Reform" in Chambéry. Among the seven, Maistre and three others "had the full and unlimited confidence of Lyon."[1] These four would soon become the heart of La Sincérité, a reformed Scottish rite lodge established in April 1778 and dependent on the College Metropolitain de Lyon. They and twelve other Brothers were officially transferred from Trois Mortier to La Sincérité on September 4, 1778.

The grades (or degrees) of the new lodge, established by Willermoz, were Apprenti, Compagnon, and Maître, followed by the higher grades, Maître Ecossais de Saint-Andre, Ecuyer novice, and CBCS (mentioned above). In addition, Willermoz added a pair of even higher grades, the Profès and the Grand Profès, which were theoretically unknown to members of the CBCS grade. Willermoz placed the new lodge, along with other lodges affiliated with Lyon, under the German obedience of the Stricte Observance Templiére, whose Grand Master was Prince Ferdinand of Brunswick, to whom Maistre would write a famous memoir in 1782.

Although a member and soon-to-be Grand Profès of La Sincérité, Maistre was influenced by others besides Willermoz, among them Martinès de Pasqually (1727–1774) and Louis-Claude de Saint-Martin (whose influence on Maistre has been mentioned). Pasqually's movement, though not Masonic, had long been attractive to those who frequented Masonic circles. Flamboyantly called the Ordre des Chevalier Maçons Elus Cöen de L'Universe (Order of the Knight Masons, Elected Priests of the Universe), it taught the reintegration of created entities into the Creator and a system of grades influenced by Willermoz. For his part, Saint-Martin influenced Maistre mostly through his elegant theosophical and illuminist writings, which condemned the *philosophes* for undermining religious faith and, at one point, proposed to hasten the coming of the reign of Christ by concentrated meditation on the Bible. In *L'homme de désir* (mentioned in the last chapter), he maintained "that it was man's desire and that of God to achieve mystical unity."[2] As we have seen, Maistre was especially influenced by this work, in which the regenerated and

---

1. Antoine Faivre, "Maistre and Willermoz," in *Maistre Studies*, 127.
2. Lebrun, *Joseph de Maistre: An Intellectual Militant*, 68.

initiated "man of desire" was instructed in all manner of theosophical messages and spiritual invocations. Patterned after the Psalms, the clear, gracefully written work discussed meditation on spirits and angels, verbal and silent prayer, original sin, sacrifice, and expiation, and the role of the poet as prophet. These writings of the "philosophe inconnu" (unknown philosopher), an Elus Cöen by Pasqually's initiation, would inspire, deepen, and solace the Savoyard in the years ahead.

Returning now to Maistre and Willermoz, we discover a certain tension in the relationship between these two men of forceful personality. According to Antoine Faivre, Willermoz found the younger man to be not only an ardent but an "inconvenient" disciple, a fact that testifies to the master's firm sense of authority and to Maistre's critical intelligence, seriousness of purpose, and refusal to accept doctrine that was not fully explained. In a letter to Willermoz of June 1779, Maistre expressed a measure of doubt about the origins of the texts which contained the instructions for the Profès and the Grands Profès. In response, Willermoz urged confidence on the part of his disciple, assuring him that the teaching "offered a chain of which all the links are in place" and an explanation of the "intellectual and physical universe." Furthermore, Willermoz claimed, the teaching was able to demonstrate Maistre's unity with "all the relations that link you in this quality with the rest of the universe and its author."[3] Such a sweeping assertion was in keeping with the integrative potentials of esotericist doctrine in general, of that form of thought in which individuals or groups of initiates—be they theosophists, alchemists, Rosicrucians, Masons, or gnostics of various types—had explored the arcane and mysterious inner realities of religion, cosmology, and metaphysics from time immemorial.

Maistre was most likely delighted to find himself, according to the doctrine of Willermoz, demonstrably linked or integrated into this larger pattern of nature and supernature. However, his doubts drew the displeasure of the master. On a stern note, Willermoz informed the young Grand Profès that he would withhold additional proofs until such time as Maistre had been further nourished by the read-

---

3. Faivre, "*Maistre and Willermoz*," 128.

ings that had already been confided to him. Undeterred, Maistre followed up with additional letters, indicating continuing doubts. In light of these further queries, Willermoz concluded that Maistre had been admitted too quickly to the higher grades, and thus had been unable to assimilate its wisdom by gradual preparation.

Gradual preparation aside, it would appear the Count's earnest quest for intellectual truth was at the root of his badgering of Willermoz. In the words of Antoine Faivre, "For the faculty of sensing certain truths, Joseph de Maistre [had] substituted that of examining them coldly with his intelligence." Such was characteristic of the man. Whether analyzing the politics of revolution or pondering the arcana of illuminism, he was wont to bring his prodigious intellect to bear on the matter at hand. Unlike the caricature of the dogmatic, close-minded reactionary that has been sketched so often, Maistre was a man of supple mind, with a large measure of critical intelligence. However much he might have wished that lesser mortals would accept the hoary wisdom of the race—or the teaching of an illuminist master—on the say-so of constituted authority, he was at times far from willing to do so himself. That being said, he met his match in Willermoz, who stood firm in his principles, convinced that he possessed a revelation that completed the official teaching of the churches. In the end, Maistre remained loyal to Willermoz, conceding at last the master's right to teach from the spirit that informed his metaphysical intelligence. "Here my pen falls," Maistre said, "and, full of respect and with confidence toward my masters, I wait their decision without anticipating them."[4] This concession largely closed the circle that bound the doctrines of the two men. In spite of whatever disagreements might have remained, they were as one in practicing the Catholic faith, in insisting the Masonic regime must remain Christian, and in believing the esoteric sciences were an excellent means of deepening the dogmas of Christianity.

That which can be said of Maistre regarding Catholicism and Masonry can be said of Masonry in Chambéry more generally. In addition to the fashionable aspect of belonging to a lodge, more than a few members were drawn for weightier reasons, as they

4. Ibid., 129–31.

found the churches spiritually mediocre and ill-suited to the mentality of the age. Researchers have discovered "the importance of spiritual motivations and preoccupations" among Masons of the period, especially in Templar and other occultist obediences such as the Scottish Reform.[5] Though the Catholic Church had formally opposed Freemasonry since 1738, its displeasure failed to discourage even its most devoted sons from participation in the lodges.

On a more prosaic note, a glimpse of Maistre's Masonic associations is provided by Friedrich Münter, noted scholar, churchman, and Mason, who was passing through Chambéry in February 1787. Münter recorded in his diary that he was taken to meet "a certain Count Maistre, an assistant of the Senate, a young man and well informed." While spending the next two evenings together, they "recognized each other as brothers, ate together at an inn, and talked of Masonry and other things." The second of the two meetings was spent at Maistre's home, where additional brothers were present and conversation turned again to Masonry. The following morning, Münter was present when Maistre "magnetized" a friend who was suffering from gout. This practice, in vogue at the time, was an esoterically-tinged medical technique, first made popular by Friedrich Mesmer, the pioneer hypnotist. According to Richard Lebrun, "This is the only evidence we have that Maistre was interested in magnetism, but there is no reason to doubt its veracity…we know that one of Maistre's friends, Dr. Sebastien Giraud, also a high ranking Mason, was a great advocate of the practice."[6]

René Guénon, well over a century later, viewed Masonry in much the same way as Maistre. As a young man exploring the occult underworld of Paris, he had been drawn to fringe Masonic groups owing to the overlap between these and other esoteric groups to which he belonged. Though he discovered bogus rites and dubious chiefs in certain of these groups, Guénon nevertheless believed Masonry—at its best—to be a repository of rites and symbols in which echoes of its initiatory past could still be detected. And despite opposition from the Catholic Church, he was convinced that

---

5. Jean-Louis Darcel, "Sources of Maistrian Sensibility," in *Maistre Studies*, 115.
6. Lebrun, 69.

Masonry's link to the Primordial Tradition, from which he maintained all valid spiritualities had derived, made of it the remnant of a once thriving entity.

Moreover, he held that Masonry had fallen away from its original initiatory and symbolic heritage in much the same way as the Catholic Church had from its. In Guénon's view, a restored Masonry—shorn of its political and anti-clerical elements—could remind the church of the esoteric and initiatory aspects that had been displaced. Though in the end his vision was not realized, his influence was not entirely absent, inasmuch as La Grande Loge Nationale Francaise granted his views serious attention. (*The Great Triad*, a lodge founded to study his book of the same name, was less well received and lasted only a short time.) At the very least, according to Robin Waterfield, Guénon "reopened a door long closed and reminded Masons of the true initiatory nature and function of their brotherhood."[7]

Not surprisingly, Guénon referenced Maistre's Masonic writings in his own work. Of particular interest is a review of Maistre's 1782 *Mémoire*—or memorandum—to Duke Ferdinand of Brunswick, Grand-Master of the Rectified Scottish Rite (see below). In the *Mémoire*, Maistre had responded to a questionnaire sent by the duke to all the lodges of his obedience in preparation for the Convent of Wilhelmsbad. Maistre's reply is the most important piece of writing to emerge from his early years, though it is doubtful the duke ever read it.

The *Mémoire au duc de Brunswick*, to give it its full title, was colored by the teachings of Willermoz, and included Maistre's concession that the Lyon master had indeed the right to teach from the spirit that informed his metaphysical intelligence, as observed above. In the *Mémoire* overall, the young initiate waxed eloquent on the potentials of esoteric Masonry. "What a vast field is open to the zeal and perseverance of the G.P. [Grand Profès]," he wrote. "Would that some of them penetrate courageously into the erudite studies that can multiply our titles and explain those we possess. Would that

7. Robin Waterfield, *René Guénon and the Future of the West* (San Rafael, CA, 2002: Sophia Perennis), 124.

still others [such as Willermoz] ... tell us what they have learned from the Spirit, who blows where He wills, as He wills, and when He wills."[8]

Also in the *Mémoire,* Maistre proposed three grades of Masonry. The first would promote among its members benevolent acts and the study of morals and politics; the second would promote reunion of the Christian churches and sects—a goal dear to Maistre's heart—as well as instruction in government, and the third would seek the "revelation of revelation," the "sublime knowledge" that constitutes "knowledge of man" at the highest level, a "transcendent Christianity" based on factual research and metaphysical knowledge.[9] One cannot but detect in this three-fold scheme a trace of the Gnosticism present in the early centuries of the Christian church, a view in which humanity was divided into three basic types: the hylic, who was material only, lacking faith and spiritual knowledge; the psychic, who had faith but still lacked spiritual knowledge; and the pneumatic, who possessed spiritual knowledge (gnosis, illumination). These seem to roughly correspond to the types and tasks Maistre assigned to his Masonic grades, and parallel also the division into castes and classes present in traditional societies.

Though disposed favorably toward the work of esoteric Masonry, the ever-vigilant Count found a measure of irony and humor amidst its solemn purposes. In the *Mémoire,* he intimated as much.

There is perhaps not a single mason, if somewhat able to think, who has not asked himself within one hour of his reception "What is the origin of all that I see? Whence come these strange ceremonies, this pomp, these grand words, etc...?" But after having lived some time in the Order, one asks other questions: "What is the origin of these mysteries which veil nothing, of these types which represent nothing? Lo! Men of all countries will meet (and perhaps have done so for several centuries) to rank on two lines, swear never to reveal a secret which does not exist, put their right hand to their left shoulder, draw it to the right one, and sit down to table. Can't they talk nonsense, eat and drink to excess, without

8. Lebrun, 62–66.
9. Faivre, 130.

discoursing about Hiram and Solomon's Temple, the Blazing Star, etc., etc…?"[10]

In poking fun at certain aspects of Masonry, Maistre expressed his characteristic independence of mind, a willingness to keep at least some distance between his speculative allegiances and his critical faculties. But despite the evidence of such lighter passages, he respected—and greatly needed—the compensating balance provided by this esoteric and fraternal pursuit. Maistre the Catholic, imbued with a sense of duty and pessimism, must have found the camaraderie of Masonry, alongside its esoteric doctrines, a welcome departure from his strictly religious meditations.

Masonry and Catholicism, moreover, could be said to share many ideas, a cross-fertilization that delighted and reassured Maistre. These ideas, according to Richard Lebrun, included "a Providential interpretation of history, the solidarity of men before God, original sin, the idea of the reversibility of merits whereby the innocent suffer for the guilty, the necessity and efficacy of sacrifice, the desire for a mystical experience of God, [and] hope for a reunion of all Christians." In consequence, Maistre lauded Masonry and celebrated its rise to prominence during the heyday of Enlightenment hegemony. "It is as surprising and extraordinary," he wrote to the Baron Vignet des Etoles in 1793, "that at the moment when skepticism appears to me to have exterminated the religious verities in all of Europe, there should arise everywhere societies who have no other aim or occupation than the study of religion."[11]

Thanks to Freemasonry, Maistre belonged to just such a society. Lodge and parish—complementing one other—were married in his soul. He was a student and adherent of religion, but compelled by a measure of aridity in the contemporary religious climate, combined with the austere and moralistic tenor of much of his early training, to look for sustenance at least partly outside of ecclesial structures, even while remaining loyal to the church.

In reviewing the *Mémoire*, René Guénon expressed a mixed view

10. Edmond Mazet, "Freemasonry and Esotericism," in *Modern Esoteric Spirituality*, 263–64.
11. Lebrun, *Throne and Altar*, 119–20.

of Maistre's work on this subject. On the one hand, he faulted him for failure to accept the Templar origin of Masonry, for misunderstanding the concept of "Unknown Superiors," and for an imperfect initiation despite his high grade in Masonry. In commenting on Maistre's opinion that the destruction of the Templars was of little significance, he begged to differ. "[I]t matters very much," Guénon wrote, "since this marks the point at which the West broke with its own initiatic tradition . . . a rupture that is truly the primary cause of the intellectual deviation of the modern world."[12]

On the other hand, Guénon took into consideration Maistre's age at the time he wrote and the conditions of Masonry at the time he lived. On balance, he found certain strengths in the author's inspired effort, including his contention that the initiation of which Masonry is heir goes back "to the origin of things," to the beginning of the world. "The true religion"—he is quoting Maistre—"spans far more than eighteen centuries: it was born the day that days were born."[13] He also credits Maistre's view that Masonry embodies "a great psychological truth"[14] in its insistence on rituals and oath-taking, aspects vital to cultivating the right spirit among its members.

There is little indication that Maistre's interest in Masonry waned during his long years at the court of the tzar, 1803–1817, but his full approval appears to have diminished. His greatest work, the *Soirées de St. Pétersbourg*, injects a note of ambiguity regarding Masonry—and illuminism more broadly—in ways we do not see in previous writings. Conceived as early as 1810 but published only in 1822, the year following the author's death, the *Soirées* is a masterpiece of unresolved discussion, not least in regard to illuminism. Displaying a genius for the dialogue form, Maistre structured the work as a series of conversations between a Chevalier (the Knight), a Comte (the Count, representing Maistre) and a Sénateur (the Senator). This verbally animated trio was used to analyze the baffling problem of pain and evil in a world purportedly created and governed by a loving God, a theme which allowed Maistre to ring the changes on

12. Guénon, *Studies in Freemasonry*, 123.
13. Ibid.
14. Ibid., 125.

theodicy in ways new and old. Depending on which of the three men is speaking, it is either critical or praiseworthy of illuminism.

According to the Count, the illuminism taught by Saint-Martin and related thinkers centered on the pursuit of "supernatural knowledge." They did not doubt, he says, "that it is possible for men to put themselves in communication with the spiritual world, to have commerce with the spirits, and thus to discover the rarest mysteries."[15] Unlike the Maistre of earlier days, the Count finds "commerce" of this kind to be troubling, for such communications—if truly accessible to the illuminist adept—would soon become no more than everyday prodigies, miraculous and revelatory manifestations diverting men from the more important tasks of achieving an elevated morality and piety. On a positive note, however, he credits Masonry for its influence in Protestant lands, where he says it is useful in maintaining religious feeling, accustoming the mind to dogma and countering the effects of the Reformation, hence preparing the way for eventual reunion with Catholicism.

That being said, the Count observes there are forms of illuminism that are justifiably objectionable from the Catholic point of view. These are the non-Christian forms, often allied with rationalism and revolution, which he dismisses out of hand. Yet even Christian illuminism, he admits, can pose a danger to Catholic countries. The danger, he believes, is due less to the specific teachings of the system than to a tendency to disturb the exclusivist principles of unity and authority upon which Catholic social order is based. Nevertheless, such potential danger never caused him to abandon totally the insights of illuminist speculation.

Despite the cooling of Maistre's sympathies, the *Soirées* are allowed in part to affirm Masonry and other forms of illuminism. In the Eleventh Dialogue one finds the Senator extolling illuminism and defending it in the context of supernatural revelation, chiefly of a prophetic nature. In response to the Count's attacks, he asks for a definition to separate the varieties of *illuminé* one from another. Are they, he asks, "these guilty men in Germany who have dared in our time to conceive and even to organize . . . the frightful project of stamping out Christianity and sovereignty in Europe?" Or, he continues, are they "the virtuous disciples of Saint-Martin, who not only profess Christianity, but work only to raise themselves to the most sublime heights of this divine law?" He ruminates on the related mysteries of revelation and faith, and the need for "lofty speculation" and prophecy regarding the signs of the times. He challenges the Count's incredulity regarding the supernatural claims of Masons and other illuminists, asking him if he is not just as likely to find passages of Scripture equally improbable, though accepting them on the authority of the church. Can he, for example, read the first chapter of Genesis, or the Apocalypse, or the Song of Songs, or Ecclesiastes, without difficulty? A "thousands expressions" in Scripture, he says,

> will prove to you that it pleased God, sometimes to let men speak … according to the reigning ideas of such and such an epoch, and sometimes to hide high mysteries not made for all eyes under apparently simple and at times vulgar forms. Now…what harm is there in mining these depths of grace and divine goodness just as we mine the earth for gold or diamonds? More than ever, gentlemen, we must devote ourselves to these lofty speculations, for we must hold ourselves ready for an immense event in the divine order. . . . There is no more religion on earth, and humanity cannot remain in this state. Moreover, formidable prophets are announcing that *the time has come*.[16]

Here, the Senator recommends attention to the prophets of the age, be they devotees of illuminism or other forms of esoteric discourse; prophets who foresee extraordinary events on the horizon, events that will shake the foundations of irreligious Europe.

The task of the Mason or theosophist, then, is to exercise esoteric insight in quest of special revelation, to find in difficult and mysterious sacred texts the answers to his deepest questions, and to then attempt an exegesis. He is free to probe the "high mysteries not made for all eyes." He is encouraged to excavate the "depths of grace and divine goodness" that lie in Scripture like stones and metals in the earth, deep and precious treasures hidden from the profane.

16. Ibid., 321–22.

Over the decades, Catholicism spoken with a Masonic accent had eased the tensions of Maistre's double nature; even in his later years he could not abandon all ties to this esoteric synthesis. In a dossier labeled "illuminés," located in the family archives, he summed up his experience in the world of Masonry: "I once consecrated a good deal of my time to getting to know these gentlemen. I frequented their assemblies ... I maintained a certain correspondence with some of their principal personages. But I remained in the ... Roman Church; not however without having acquired many ideas from which I have profited."[17]

17. Lebrun, *Intellectual Militant*, 69.

4

Maistre and the Counter-Enlightenment

FOR TWO DECADES, Joseph de Maistre led the life of a dutiful public servant, eminently loyal to throne and altar but open to moderate reform in the political life of Savoy. The world historic events in France changed all of that. Maistre watched as the Revolution became increasingly radical and violent, unleashing as it did so the unholy passions of a people uprooted from the traditions of centuries. The *dénouement* is the well-known litany of regicide, civil war, the "Great Terror," and the Thermidorian Reaction, with all the well-known players on stage: Girondins, Jacobins, the committee of public safety, and the busy "national razor" dispatching enemies of the state. Maistre emerged from it all a different man. Finding himself an impoverished exile in a much-altered world, he was stung into a new kind of traditional consciousness. Thus he was equipped and inspired to articulate a vision of Counter-Enlightenment more penetrating than anyone else on the scene.

In doing so, his lively pen analyzed not only the Revolution itself but its theoretical antecedents, located especially in the writings of Voltaire and Rousseau and, further back, in the watershed philosophy of Francis Bacon. For support of his own views, he reached into the past also, especially to the Cambridge Platonists and their leading light, Ralph Cudworth, whose criticisms of Calvinist views and opposition to atheistic determinism pleased Maistre greatly. In response to the *philosophes* and their precursors, Maistre hammered out a philosophical edifice of his own, constructed unsystematically yet coherent and integrated nonetheless. In one sense, the work was uniquely his own, leavened with shrewd and esoteric insight; in the other it drew on the sagacity of the ages, from antiquity to modernity.

Maistre took aim at a variety of well-known and much heralded figures past and present. Rome was not built in a day, nor did the philosophy of Enlightenment spring fully formed on the world. It had predecessors aplenty, and Maistre meant to track them down and expose them, to critique their deficient views, and to hold them accountable for the damage that occurred in their wake. As mentioned above, Francis Bacon was among the targets, though Maistre's work on the "father of empiricism" remained unpublished until 1836, fifteen years after his death. Nonetheless, it provides a glimpse into his mature thinking from 1809, when he began the work.

In casting Bacon as a historically pivotal and largely—if unintentionally—malevolent figure, Maistre targeted one of the most celebrated of the proto-modernists, both then and now.[1] *An Examination of the Philosophy of Bacon* attacked the Lord Chancellor on a number of fronts. Inasmuch as he was touted by the *philosophes* for his inductive method and materialistic bias, he was made to order for Maistre, whose acerbic and detailed critique would be fulsomely praised by the nineteenth century literary critic Saint-Beuve, among others. Despite disagreements with Maistre on most other questions, Saint-Beuve thought the *Examination's* chapters "on final causes and on the union of religion and science contained ... certainly some of the finest pages that have ever been written in a human language."[2] More recently, scholars have come to consider this neglected work one of Maistre's most original, a showcase of polemical skill and a key to the author's epistemology.

Though Maistre was an Anglophile; though he admired Bacon's *Essays*; though he and Bacon shared a training in law, and though both were royalists largely opposed to political or social innovation, the agreements extended no further. The fundamental divide was philosophical, drawn between the theories of innate ideas and sense experience, with Maistre emphasizing the first and Bacon, along

1. Interestingly, Maistre's view is at variance with that of René Guénon, who allotted the primary role to an equally celebrated figure, René Descartes, who, ironically, received mostly praise from Maistre (see below).

2. *An Examination of the Philosophy of Bacon: Wherein Different Questions of Rational Philosophy Are Treated*, trans. and ed. Richard A. Lebrun (Montreal & Kingston, London, Buffalo: McGill-Queen's University Press, 1998), x.

with later figures such as John Locke, the second. In Maistre's view, the notion that all ideas derive from the senses was to materialize their origin and thus to reduce them to material causes, a concept he utterly rejected.

Innate ideas were to Maistre the fundamental notions or ideas common to all men, the notions or ideas that prefigure and determine all others. Thus he believed that human beings react to sense experience in ways determined by innate ideas, and that all real understanding is based on first principles. If one discounts first principles, he argued, truth is unverifiable in the metaphysical or theological domains. For lacking first principles—that is, lacking anterior, self-evident, non-derived truths—no incontrovertible proof can be deduced outside the material realm. Put otherwise, he held that every rational belief was founded on prior knowledge, for man can learn nothing but what he already knows in part. All sound reasoning, he believed, proceeded from already known principles; it was a sort of recollection.

In Maistre's view, the inert matter of contemporary physics could not be the cause of anything, yet Bacon had proposed that it was. By doing so, he had limited all real knowledge to the physical sciences, leaving men with a prejudice against and even a distaste for other kinds of knowledge. Thus theology, for example, was confined by Bacon to the church and forbidden to venture forth. Physics was the only legitimate science, and that anyone should have the temerity to mix religion and science—as had Paracelsus, scoffed Bacon—was to commit a fundamental blunder. Thus theology was reduced to mere opinion while science was enthroned as definitive. Henceforth science—empirical science, that is—found itself established as the broker of what was true and false, and with the passing of time this prejudice percolated throughout European society at every level.

Unlike the moderate tone he used regarding Bacon in the *Soirées*, Maistre was more forcible, personal, and passionate in his remarks in the *Examination*. He began the second chapter, "Of the Soul," with the following accusation: "Every line of Bacon leads to materialism, but nowhere does he show himself a more able sophist, a more refined, more profound, and more dangerous hypocrite than in what he wrote on the soul." He followed up this broadside by observing that Bacon had opened the subject in keeping with "his invariable custom, by insulting all who preceded him, and, always putting an image in the place of reason."[3]

Maistre elaborated by citing the words of Moses in Genesis chapter one, in which man is declared to be created in the image of God, created, according to Maistre, as "intelligence"—as vicegerent of the created order—after which Moses stopped, "for he ha[d] said everything." Bacon, by contrast, had no wish to stop there, but instead asserted that God had raised up man from the "slime of the earth," thereby (in Bacon's view) conflating body and soul in such a way that the physical entity with its sensible soul could become the object of science and philosophy, while the intellectual soul was relegated to the periphery of things. Regarding the sensible soul, then, sacred theology—again in Bacon's view—"meddles little, and . . . is permitted to say whatever one wants." This, while the sensible soul shared by men and animals alike, was henceforth to dominate the emancipated mind of science.[4] The "bad marriage" of theology and philosophy had been dissolved, its mismatched partners forever divided.

In pursuing a related subject, Maistre charged that Bacon was without excuse in contradicting a "great truth," one declared from the pen of the empiricist himself, to wit, "[T]hat religion is the spice that prevents science from corrupting itself."[5] Thus Bacon's lopsided materialism, Maistre said, stood "not only against the truth, but also against his conscience, in according to the natural sciences a supremacy that in no way belongs to them."[6] Whence the contradiction? Was Bacon a hypocrite? It is a possibility, it seems, for he was a mix of varied qualities: artful, cautious, flattering, venal, Machiavellian, materialistic, skeptical, deistic, Protestant, Jesuitical. Maistre toyed with the idea of hypocrisy before discarding it, concluding instead that Bacon simply did not know his own mind. In

3. Ibid., 172.
4. Ibid., 175.
5. Ibid., 271. It appears that Bacon never said this verbatim, but it can be reconstructed from his expression of similar sentiments.
6. *Examination*, 271.

attempting to distinguish true from false, he surmised, Bacon merely spoke his thoughts of a moment, dancing around the truth to disguise his real motives and meaning.

This was never more true than in *The Characters of a Believing Christian*, a work replete with apparent contradiction if not downright confusion. Maistre pointed to an especially egregious example, wherein Bacon had written: "He [the Christian] is sometimes so troubled that he think nothing to be true in religion: yet, if he did think so, he could not at all be troubled." Commenting on such "gibberish," Maistre believed it to be "the written image of what existed in Bacon's head. Deprived of fixed principles on all points, and having in mind only negations, between ancient belief and new reform, between authority and revolt, between Plato and Epicurus, he ended by not even knowing what he knew."[7]

That Maistre took critical aim at Francis Bacon is no surprise, but that he held a mostly favorable view of René Descartes is, for in this he stands in contrast to the view of René Guénon, as noted above. Scholars have long pondered why Maistre assigned such blame to Bacon (and Locke) for their influence on eighteenth century thought, while passing over the earlier Cartesian contribution to mechanistic and materialistic views. Maistre, who possessed a variety of Descartes's writings, nearly always showed great deference to him, though he seldom cited him firsthand. According to Richard Lebrun, even though modern scholarship locates Descartes at the origins of modernity and stresses "the contribution of the 'material' side of Cartesian dualism," it appears that for Maistre and certain of his co-religionists Descartes remained "an undoubtedly Catholic thinker." Maistre also accorded him high status as a great mathematician and scientist—in contrast to the less gifted Bacon—and as an authority who rightly opposed the sensible origin of ideas.[8]

To Guénon, by contrast, it was Descartes who played the lead role in the transition to a recognizably modern science. Not that Guénon totally ignored Bacon, but his citations of the Englishman are scattered and brief, mostly mentioning him in conventional terms for

7. Ibid., 301.
8. Ibid., xxix.

his obvious influence on the direction of science.[9] Perhaps Guénon focused more on Descartes because he was a fellow countryman, and thus more familiar to him. Be that as it may, it was his view that Descartes was the first to apply rationalism to the scientific field, thus introducing a variety of mechanism to the European mind for the first time since the ancients, when the atomistic ideas of Democritus and Epicurus expressed a type of mechanistic thinking.

In the philosophy of Descartes, Guénon asserted, the mind was a thinking, non-extended thing, wholly distinct from the body, which was a non-thinking but extended thing. "The truth is," Guénon said, "that materialism merely represents one of the two halves of Cartesian dualism, the half to which its author had applied the mechanistic conception; it was sufficient thereafter [in the minds of many] to ignore or to deny the remaining half, or, what comes to the same thing, to claim to bring the whole of reality into the first half, in order to arrive quite naturally at materialism."[10] Hence Descartes's position, regardless of his intent, was interpreted to mean the human being was more or less reduced to the body alone, in keeping with the theory of "animal-machines." As a result of Descartes's mind-body dualism, then, and owing to the large number of persons prepared and eager to entertain material explanations alone, the mental half became something of a "useless complication." Henceforth the rational mind was increasingly treated as non-existent for all practical purposes. In this development, Guénon (and others) identified one of the great ruptures in the history of European thought, one that increasingly saw quantity not quality, substance not essence, to be the end-all and be-all of philosophical and, in particular, scientific investigation.

Though Maistre largely missed the problematical implications of Cartesian thought for the future direction of European philosophy, there was another Frenchman, of more immediate awareness to him, who readily typified all that he saw as wrongheaded and dan-

---

9. He also mentioned a curious belief of the Theosophical Society, in which Bacon appears as a reincarnated "Master."

10. *The Reign of Quantity and the Signs of the Times* (Ghent, NY: Sophia Perennis et Universalis, 1995), 118–19.

gerous. François-Marie Arouet—Voltaire, of course—met with the Savoyard's deepest scorn. Labeling him a pernicious mountebank, Maistre mocked Voltaire's self-presentation as a persecuted man of letters and noble martyr, when in fact this celebrated *litterateur* lived in a grand house at Ferney, receiving visitors and admirers, surrounded by servants and friends, and savoring his reputation as the most famous writer in Europe. To Maistre, the exile and actual martyr (in the sense of "witness"), a man separated from home and family, such pretensions were intolerable. According to a recent assessment, one could sense in this attitude "both Maistre's resentment of, and feeling of superiority toward, the literary icon of Enlightenment."[11]

In estimating Voltaire's brilliant and malicious wit, his tireless insistence on progressive reforms, and his scathing attacks on the Catholic Church, Maistre judged him to be—along with Jean-Jacques Rousseau—one of the two most powerful influences in creating the climate for revolution in France. "Voltaire's corrosive writings," Maistre declared, "gnawed for sixty years at the very Christian cement of this superb structure whose fall has startled Europe." So too did the corrosive work of the equally culpable Rousseau, who, in Maistre's view, applied his eloquence to seduce the crowd of those "over which imagination has more purchase than reason." Less rationalistic than Voltaire, he asserted, the sentimentalist Rousseau "breathed everywhere scorn for authority and the spirit of insurrection." It was he "who traced the code of anarchy, and who, in the midst of some isolated and sterile truths that everyone before him knew, posed the disastrous principles of which the horrors we have seen are only the immediate consequences."[12]

Maistre's view of Rousseau was more complicated than his view of Voltaire but his criticism was equally trenchant. Though the

11. Douglas Hedley, "Enigmatic Images of an Invisible World: Sacrifice, Suffering and Theodicy in Joseph de Maistre," in *Joseph de Maistre and the Legacy of Enlightenment*, ed. Carolina Armenteros and Richard A. Lebrun (University of Oxford: Voltaire Foundation, 2011), 129.

12. Maistre, *Against Rousseau: "On the State of Nature" and "On the Sovereignty of the People,"* trans. Richard A. Lebrun (Montreal & Kingston, London, Buffalo: McGill-Queen's University Press, 1996), 106.

votaries of the two men celebrated the "power" they exercised over their century, Maistre lamented it. "Yes, they were powerful," he remarked, "like poisons and fires."[13] He took special aim at Rousseau's "state of nature" arguments, observing that even Voltaire criticized the primitivism and sentimentalism of Rousseau's assertion that the earliest men were discouraged from harming one another by a sort of fellow feeling, living as they did in the simplest of conditions. According to Rousseau, it was only later, as the confining structures of civilization were developed, that the competition for property and status corrupted the estimable morals of primitive man. Such tribes as had remained in a primitive state, he said, were the remnants of the earliest period of human society, and examples of rudimentary but real virtue.

Maistre begged to differ. "J.J. Rousseau," he declared, "one of the most dangerous sophists of his age and yet the most bereft of true knowledge, wisdom, and above all profundity, having an apparent depth that is entirely a matter of words," was guilty of taking contemporary "savages" as examples of primitive man, whereas they were in fact nothing other than the descendants of some individual man, unknown to history, and now "detached from the great tree of civilization by some transgression. . . . I doubt if new savages can be created." As a result of the same error, Maistre said, there were some who believed the languages of contemporary primitives were the original languages of the race. To the contrary, Maistre charged, they were none other than "the debris of ancient languages, *ruined*, as it were, and degraded like the men who speak [them]." There is, he said, an *"original illness* just as there is an *original sin*," by virtue of which members of the human race—civilized and uncivilized alike—are subject to all kinds of suffering, degradation and vice.[14]

In developing his views on Rousseau's theories of the state of nature, social contract, and sovereignty of the people, Maistre demonstrated an evolution in his own thinking. Written in 1794–95 (but unpublished until 1870, almost fifty years after his death), Maistre's

13. Ibid.
14. *The Saint Petersburg Dialogues*, in *The Works of Joseph de Maistre*, trans. Jack Lively, 196–97.

two essays on Rousseau reflected the move from a largely political interpretation of the origins and nature of the French Revolution, held prior to the Revolution itself, to the providential interpretation that marked his major writings after the event. They also confirmed his rejection of earlier affinities and ambiguities in his assessment of Rousseau's thought, for by the time of these writings he had become decidedly hostile to the Genevan's views. Years earlier, Maistre had employed a vocabulary, literary style, and "sensibility" suggesting Rousseau's influence when he delivered a "Discourse on Virtue" to the Senate of Savoy in 1777, and he had quoted the "eloquent Rousseau" with approval as late as 1788, but by the time of his later essays he had taken a highly critical and polemical tone. "The best way to refute this so-called philosopher," he suggested in the 1790s, "is to analyze him and translate him into philosophical language; then we are surprised we have ever been able to give him a moment's attention."[15]

Yet even after revising his opinion, Maistre continued to express ideas not wholly alien to his adversary. For example, Maistre's belief in perfectibility as a human possibility (albeit by God's grace, and despite severe imperfections at present) resonated with Rousseau's view of human development over extended periods of time. The two men also shared a measure of agreement about the nature of the political problem, including the idea that the state is a necessary remedy for human failings. In treating of these failings, however, Rousseau had repudiated the Christian explanation of original sin while Maistre believed it explained "everything." Maistre also differed in his contention that the social order is the natural order for human life, whereas Rousseau declared that contemporary society was unnatural and that it was man's social development that was to blame for his miseries and discontents.[16]

Elsewhere, Maistre's attack on Rousseau's anthropology of primitive innocence brought to mind a citation from Epictetus, who warned the man "who wants to advance toward perfection to distrust himself *like an enemy and a traitor.*" Thus the most excellent

---

15. *Against Rousseau*, xii–xiii.
16. Ibid., xiv–xv.

moralist, Maistre stated, would have been correct to say "that *the great goal of all our efforts must be to render ourselves stronger than ourselves.*" On these and related points, he asserted, Rousseau could not and did not contradict the "universal conscience" nor the plain fact that men are wicked. Here, Rousseau allowed, "*sad and continual experience spares the need for proof.*" Yet despite this concession, he still held that man is "naturally good," and claimed he had demonstrated the fact. Maistre called this notion laughable before stripping it and putting it in the form of a syllogism: "*Man is naturally good, if his vices do not derive from his nature. Moreover, all the vices of man come from society, which is against nature: therefore man is naturally good.*" On this "pile of sand," Maistre charged, Rousseau built the shaky structures of the *Discourse on Inequality, Emile,* and part of the *Social Contract.* Observing that Rousseau elsewhere demonstrated a "more reasonable" view in asserting that man contains within himself two distinct principles, the one good and the other evil, Maistre finds even this insight failed to curb the Genevan's folly. "I will not," he wrote, "examine the pitiful conclusion that Rousseau draws from this observation; it would only prove that he never saw anything but the surface of objects."[17]

In combating the ideas of Rousseau, Voltaire, and the *philosophes* at large, Maistre had recourse to any number of traditional sources, but none delighted and profited him more than the works of the Cambridge Platonists of the seventeenth century. Here, Ralph Cudworth's *The True Intellectual System of the Universe,* with which he had been familiar since his youth, ranked first in his affections. Not only did he enlist Cudworth in his counter-Enlightenment projects, but his earliest Masonic writings also indicated attentive reading of Cudworth's famous work. When Maistre fled Savoy in the wake of the French invasion of 1792, *The True Intellectual System* was among the few volumes he chose to save from his library.

In addition to relishing their congenial metaphysics, Maistre found the Cambridge Platonists of particular help in formulating his polemics against the Enlightenment project. Their repository of arguments combined harmoniously with the skills and tempera-

17. Ibid., 35–36.

ment of a one-time magistrate. For Maistre was by nature and training a man who "drew the pen as one draws the sword," a man who could summon "all the resources of the jurist to prepare a case in favour of the fight he was undertaking." The Cambridge authors provided an abundance of such resources. Maistre also discovered these authors had been attacked by name in the *Encyclopédie*, a fact that further strengthened the bond he felt toward them. Henceforth, the Cambridge polemics became his polemics.[18]

Cudworth, who along with Henry More was the leader of the Cambridge group, appears twice in the *Soirées*. He is first mentioned near the end of the second dialogue, where the discussion turns to *sensationalism*—the view that ideas originate in the senses, as taught by John Locke and his French disciple, Condillac—and its opposite number, *innatism*. Cudworth's doctrine that no effect "is greater than its cause ... [and that] the spirit is older than the world"[19] sums up the latter view, placing spirit before matter in the traditional way. On this notion as on others, Maistre aligned himself with Cudworth and his associates, not to mention a long line of famous thinkers including Plato, Origen, St. Augustine, Descartes, and Leibniz. According to these notable savants, God had placed innate ideas and principles in the human mind, thus grounding knowledge on something more dependable than experience and the senses.[20] Maistre had little trouble in spotting the sophistry behind the contrary view, for knowledge gained from the senses presupposes the intellectual knowledge that precedes, receives, and interprets it. Yet materialists to this day, in a clear case of begging the question, continue to deny the prior and necessary role of the intellect, even as they claim objectivity for their sensory-based views.

With such polemical weapons as were provided by the Cambridge school, not to mention a raft of other resources culled from

18. Philippe Barthelet, "The Cambridge Platonists Mirrored by Joseph de Maistre," *Joseph de Maistre and the Legacy of Enlightenment*, 68.
19. Ibid., 471.
20. Members of the traditionalist school of the twentieth century, not surprisingly, hold to the same view, a view that grounds ethics and metaphysics on the basis of eternal and immutable principles, and teaches that all men have innate knowledge and awareness of God.

ancient and modern authors, Maistre found himself equipped to confront the anti-traditional *philosophes* and their theories in a variety of fields. These weapons found major expression in the 1797 work that made his reputation, *Considerations on France*, in which he analyzed the French Revolution as a work of God's providence. In doing so, Maistre saw the Revolution as a divine punishment on a nation that had betrayed its mandate to model Christian morality and sovereignty. France, he said, had "used her influence to contradict her vocation and demoralize Europe"; no one should be surprised "if she is brought back to her mission by terrible means."[21]

Reflecting on the historical record, Maistre asserted that considerable time had passed since such frightful punishments had been inflicted on a nation. In such punishments as had fallen on France, he observed, it was the guiltiest parties who suffered the most. "No doubt," he conceded, "there are innocents among the unfortunate victims, but they are far fewer than is commonly imagined." He described the guilty parties as all who had opposed the laws of property with "metaphysical sophisms"; all who counseled, approved, or favored the use of violent measures against the king; all who willed the Revolution in its destructive power and murderous inclinations. Hence many had "very justly" become its victims. "We groan to see illustrious scholars fall beneath Robespierre's axe," Maistre observed. "Humanly, we cannot be too sorry for them; but divine justice has not the least respect for geometers or physicists. Too many French scholars were the principal authors of the Revolution, too many approved and gave their support so long as the Revolution . . . struck down only the tallest heads."[22]

According to Maistre, an assault on sovereignty was among the greatest of crimes, and the execution of Louis XVI an unspeakable atrocity. As the deposed king was marched to his death, surrounded by sixty-thousand armed men, "not a voice was raised for the unfortunate monarch, and the provinces were as mute as the capital." Not only was this a crime against sovereignty, Maistre charged,

21. *Considerations on France*, trans. and ed. Richard A. Lebrun (Cambridge University Press, 1994), 9.
22. Ibid.

it was a crime against a man who had merited neither blame nor reproach. Yet the immense crowd of onlookers, civilian and soldier alike, uttered no objection to the deed that was done. "In sum," Maistre said, "never have a greater number of guilty people shared (with many gradations, to be sure) in a greater crime."[23]

Not surprisingly in such a climate of violence, the Revolution devoured its own. "Here again," Maistre observed, "we may admire order in disorder, for it is evident, if we reflect a bit, that the guiltiest revolutionaries could be felled only by the blows of their accomplices." Where had so many of them gone, he asked rhetorically. Whence Mirabeau? Bailly? Thouret? Ossellin? "One could name by the thousands the active instruments of the Revolution who have died a violent death."[24]

But were only the most guilty among the victims? By no means. "This is precisely what Providence did not want," Maistre asserted. "The great purification [he believed the Ancien Régime—its aristocracy and clergy—had indeed needed cleansing] must be accomplished and eyes must be opened; the metal of France, freed from its sour and impure dross, must emerge cleaner and more malleable into the hands of a future king."[25] Such divine alchemy, he believed, acted like a human tribunal in condemning the guilty and the innocent alike, allowing a hundred-thousand murders to cleanse a nation of its crimes and follies.

Yet in spite of its crimes—or because of them—the Revolutionary beast waxed in power. For the government "hardened the soul of France by tempering it in blood." A coalition of enemies having gathered on its borders, intent on killing the beast, found the beast impossible to kill. "What supernatural means could confound the efforts of conspiring Europe?" Maistre asked. "Only the infernal genius of Robespierre could accomplish this prodigy.... [T]he spirit of the soldiers was exasperated, and their strength was doubled by ferocious despair and contempt for life induced by rage." Hence the nation in arms—an immense host whose numbers were

23. Ibid., 11–12.
24. Ibid., 13.
25. Ibid., 14.

unprecedented—beat back the foes of France and preserved the republic. "All life, all wealth, all power was in the hands of the revolutionary authority, and this monstrous power, drunk with blood and success, the most frightful phenomenon that has ever been seen . . . was both a horrible chastisement for the French and the sole means of saving France."[26]

Yet for all its "satanic" success (Maistre believed that infernal elements had indeed prospered the Revolution) this vast and victorious enterprise was unable to evoke in the masses something as simple as a spirit of celebration. Though Christian observances—for Saint John, Saint Martin, Saint Benedict and others—had for centuries animated the people to worship and celebrate, the Revolution and its invented ceremonies had no like effect. Against the simple joys of religious festivals, Maistre said, one must compare the legislated events of "the masters of France," men invested with every power by an unprecedented revolution yet "unable to organize a simple holiday. They pour out money, they call all the arts to their assistance, and the citizens remain at home, taking notice of the call only to laugh at the organizers."[27]

In gauging the Republic's potential longevity, Maistre asked if "a durable government [could] emerge from this bloody mire?" In considering the question, he observed that barbarian peoples of savage and licentious morals had been civilized in the past, and that "barbarous ignorance" had no doubt presided over the creation of any number of political systems. But the Revolution was something else altogether. In Maistre's view, "[L]earned barbarism, systematic atrocity, calculated corruption, and, above all, irreligion have never produced anything. Greenness leads to maturity; rottenness leads to nothing."[28] He predicted the Republic was not long for this world, and in part he was right. The rise of Napoleon had already begun, and under his forthcoming regime France would become an empire with an emperor, a far cry from the spirit of 1789, yet certain elements and symbols of the Republic would be retained. Following

26. Ibid., 16.
27. Ibid., 44.
28. Ibid., 40.

Napoleon's final defeat in 1815 the Royalists would at last return to power, but France would continue to experience revolutions (less cataclysmic than the first) and frequent political instability until beyond the mid-twentieth century.

Maistre's analysis of Enlightenment philosophies and notable figures, followed by his writings on the Revolution itself, were pioneering efforts. Even as France pioneered the first modern revolution, he (alongside Edmund Burke) was first to investigate the causes of this unprecedented upheaval. In doing so, he laid down the markers by which similar upheavals could be identified in the future, for the French Revolution was only the first of many to follow. The Red and Brown revolutions of the twentieth century in Russia and Germany, respectively, mirrored their French predecessor in a variety of frightful ways, namely in their mass executions, international aggression, expropriations, political violence, and scapegoating of races, classes, and economic groups. All such reverberations recall the primal modern revolution, as do similar upheavals in countries large and small not only in Europe but among peoples around the world.

Maistre saw it all coming. "In a word," he predicted, "if there is no moral revolution in Europe, if the religious spirit is not reinforced in this part of the world, the social bond will dissolve." In the wake of further reflection, he pronounced the French Revolution "a great epoch" and predicted "that its consequences, in all kinds of ways, will be felt far beyond the time of its explosion and the limits of its birthplace."

Clearly they have been.

5

Maistre and the Catholic-Protestant Split

JOSEPH DE MAISTRE was a Roman Catholic with a difference. As in most things, he stamped his strong personal identity on an essentially orthodox and traditional teaching. In addition, he leavened his faith with Masonic affiliations, Neo-Platonic leanings, Origenist ideas,[1] and esoteric research more broadly. Despite it all, he was a born, bred, and devoted Catholic churchman, never wavering in his Christian faith.[2]

---

1. Maistre was influenced by Origen (c. 185–c. 254) more than any other theologian. He borrowed from this Alexandrian divine a number of speculative doctrines and tendencies, among them the doctrine of *apocatastasis*, which held that all men, angels, and other created beings would eventually be redeemed. Allowing that he did not intend to defend every line of Origen's writings—after all, Origen was declared a heretic two centuries after his death—Maistre upheld and internalized the Alexandrian's Biblical insights, spiritual direction, and all-around genius. To this end, he cited a favorable reference to him from the upright Bishop Bossuet and declared it was enough for him (Maistre) to chant a most Origenist clause of the liturgy, "Both the earth and the sea, and the stars themselves, all beings are washed by this blood," (Quoted from Maistre's *Eclaircissement sur les Sacrifices* [*Enlightenment on Sacrifices*] in Owen Bradley, *A Modern Maistre*, 50) to assure himself of the man's fundamental soundness. Another Origenist influence on Maistre included the doctrine of reversibility, of innocence expiating guilt, the antecedents of which were found in pagan thought and religion, and which would be linked theologically and metaphysically to the redeeming blood spilled on Calvary. Additional Origenist elements adopted to one degree or another were a pre-cosmic fall into matter and the notion that human beings had two souls within themselves, a good and celestial one and a base and terrestrial one, the latter of which resided in the blood. Maistre's Origenist theory of sacrifice, in which the remedy for an abuse arises from another abuse, and in which the existence of the bad is cosmologically justified as the auto-destruction of evil, equipped him with a providential explanation for the many calamities of life and the role they played in the expiation of sin.

2. There was a brief and quite insignificant adolescent hiatus.

A corollary of his Catholicism was a highly critical view of Protestantism, to be explored here with a nod toward René Guénon's largely parallel views. But first we must look at some length at Maistre's Catholicism itself, since it bore so heavily on his thought and manner of life. Though essentially orthodox, as intimated, we will find his faith had its eccentric qualities, qualities not absent from his method of apologetics. Moreover, despite the depth and commitment of his Catholicism, we will find also a handful of critics who question his spiritual sincerity, counter-intuitive though it might seem.

In formulating an apologetic for Catholicism, Maistre theorized—surprisingly—that the dogmas and maxims of Catholic discipline were mostly the laws of society "divinized," and sometimes "innate notions or venerable traditions sanctioned by revelation."[3] This appears at first glance to be woefully wide of the mark if one is looking at it from the perspective of theological purity. If one looks at it from the perspective of the average layman, however (or of the above-average layman in Maistre's case), it arguably reflects the reality of the tradition. If truth be told, many people of a religious turn of mind are conscientious to obey secular law and to behave in a civilized and charitable manner, but are often unaware or negligent concerning the finer points of Gospel teaching, owing to Scriptural ignorance, incomprehension, or indifference. Hence their moral awareness is mostly based on the laws of society "divinized" and the church, the Catholic Church in this case, has largely tended to content itself with this state of affairs. Always realistic, Catholicism requires most of the faithful to follow only the Ten Commandments and church dogma to attain salvation, while the minority who seek perfection follow the "evangelical counsels" (chastity, poverty, and obedience). The majority, then, find civil law in and of itself more or less congenial to their ethical sensibilities, and closely related to the religious traditions that underpin social peace and harmony.

---

3. Richard Lebrun, quoting from the Preface to the second edition of *Du Pape*, in *Throne and Altar*, 126.

Maistre and the Catholic-Protestant Split

The Maistre scholar Richard Lebrun discusses at some length the unusual approach Maistre took in defense of the faith. Maistre's method, he observes, is in fact quite different from the standard form of apologetics, from, that is, the official branch of theology that defends the faith on intellectual grounds. Instead of basing himself on the conventional Catholic sources only—divine revelation (derived from Scripture) and sacred tradition—Maistre saw himself as the inventor of a new apologetic in which, according to Lebrun, he juxtaposed religious doctrines and usages "with the necessities of the social order, the exigencies of human nature, common practices and tradition.... One may object that this is not good theology; but perhaps it would be fairer to say that it is not theology at all."[4]

Maistre acknowledged as much himself, drawing a distinction and giving a rationale for his method in *Du Pape* (*On the Pope*): "What," he asked, "has not been said on infallibility [for example] from a theological point of view! It would be difficult to add new arguments to those which the defenders of this high prerogative have assembled in order to support it."[5] Essential dogma, then, had been established a thousand times over. Maistre sensed a need for something new, with application to the issues of his time.

Hence he placed religious dogma on the one hand and human needs, human nature, and human traditions on the other, and analyzed the interplay between them. This aimed to produce "a work of controversy of a new genre which would be as convincing as any."[6] With this method he investigated auricular confession, clerical celibacy, sacrifice, papal infallibility, and divine providence. The goal was to make his writings accessible to capable but non-specialist readers. "My object," he acknowledged in a letter to M. de Place, the editor of *Du Pape*, "is to get myself read by fashionable society." In replying to a priest who had commended *Du Pape*, he indicated a wider audience: "You speak of my talent for jesting in reasoning. In

---

4. Lebrun, citing the first chapter of *Du Pape*, in *Throne and Altar*, 127.
5. Ibid.
6. Ibid., 126.

effect, I feel myself called to bring the most arduous questions to the level of every intelligence."[7]

Maistre's unorthodox method drew its share of critics. He was accused of "humanizing dogma;" of changing the reality but keeping the words; of endangering dogmas by rationalizing them, and of being a *philosophe* in spite of himself. Maistre's utilitarian defense of "national religion" caused some to question or at least comment upon his religious sincerity itself, with C. De Rémusat remarking in 1857 that "it must be acknowledged that if it [his faith] had not been sincere, he still could have written a great part of what he wrote."[8] Additional detractors have piled on. J.P. Rohden, a German, found Maistre "more theologian than Christian, more jurist than theologian," and claimed he politicized religion. The Italian, A. Omodeo, thought Maistre's religion a pretense with "only the appearance of faith." A Protestant, A. Vidalot, opined also that Maistre was not even a Christian. "In all his writings there is not a line where one senses a heart-beat, there is not a spark of Christian love." Vidalot claimed Maistre was in fact a mere child of the eighteenth century, with "its spirit, its raillery, its verve and also its skepticism. Like Voltaire, his enemy, he lacks the faith. De Maistre has only an abstract faith, he does not have the true living faith of a Christian."[9] Yet Richard Lebrun observes that Maistre's strategy to argue the political utility of religion "must be considered in the context of many other passages that argue for the sincerity of [his] religious faith."[10] We find this judgment unassailable.

Although Maistre emphasized the public value of religion, and though his personal religion was private and formal (in an age of formality, it might be noted), two persons who knew him well speak to his sincerity—if not his emotionality—in the matter of religion. According to his brother, Xavier, Joseph's habits in religion and work alike "went like the most perfect chronometer. This order and rule would seem to have to lead to dryness. But no, his heart

7. Ibid., 127.
8. Ibid., 125.
9. Ibid., 117–18.
10. Ibid., 125–27.

and mind have all their freshness." Madame Swetchine, Maistre's "illustrious convert" from the Russian church, wrote that "the idea in him ruled everything and overcame his heart, more honest and upright than naturally pious."[11] Yet pious he was. He did not wear religion on his sleeve but it was genuine nonetheless: orderly, honest, upright. "Honest" above all else. Those who read Maistre with even the slightest sympathy and know something of his life can hardly disbelieve in his religious sincerity. His conscience would not permit such hypocrisy.

Based on personal as well as public faith, then, and imbued with trust in divine providence, Maistre's religious writings were a statement of his authentic beliefs and, to a marked degree, of his personality. In keeping with his theological certitudes and personal perspective, then, it is not surprising that he stressed the somber, mysterious, and sometimes troubling aspects of Christianity. His writing served in many ways as a theodicy—as an attempt, that is, to defend the goodness and omnipotence of divine providence—to present to the reader some of the most serious and challenging aspects of the faith. In doing so, he from time to time wrote in such a way as to disturb and even shock the reader by paradox and violence of expression. (Just recall the passage about the man broken on the wheel quoted in chapter one. This was classic Maistre; he never took the easy or superficially optimistic view.) Hence there was little tender and sentimental religion in him or for his readers; it was largely the opposite. Not only did the harshest facts of life pique his interest, they stimulated some of his most vivid prose. This was manifested in his clear-eyed but poetically exaggerated style and in his choice of disturbing subject matter, as one sees in such contentions as that the executioner was the divinely appointed agent of social order; that war was "divine" in the mysterious glory that surrounds it and the attraction that draws men to it; that a man's dining table was "covered with corpses," animals slain for his nourishment and pleasure; that every disease had its source "in

11. Xavier de Maistre, quoted in *Le Correspondant* [Paris], December 1902; Madame Swetchine, quoted in Falloux du Coudray, *Life and Letters of Madame Swetchine*. Cited by Bradley in *A Modern Maistre*, 191.

some vice proscribed by Scripture" (with illnesses appropriate to anger, gluttony, incontinence, and so on). Yet he allowed also that "evils of every kind fall on humanity like bullets on an army, without distinction of persons."[12]

"Thus is worked out," Maistre continued, "from maggots up to man, the universal law of the violent destruction of living beings. The whole earth, continually steeped in blood, is nothing but an immense altar on which every living thing must be sacrificed without end, without restraint, without respite until the consummation of the world, the extinction of evil, the death of death." Whence these horrors? To what purpose? Could a benevolent but omnipotent God permit them? Theodicy demanded an answer.

Maistre had an answer and it was this: Evil is justified by the need to punish man for the primordial transgression—for the "original sin"—and for the cataract of vice and rebellion that have followed in its wake. He blended Scripture and classical philosophy to make his point. "Man is evil, horribly evil," he declared. "Has God created him like this? Emphatically no, and Plato himself hastens to reply that the good being [the divinity] neither wishes nor does evil to anyone." In examining himself, Plato had seen the corruption common to the race, and in pointing it out, saw nothing peculiar in himself, "and certainly . . . did not believe himself more evil than his fellow men." He was saying, in effect, what the psalmist David said also: "My mother has conceived me in iniquity." Elaborating this theme, Maistre contended that "every degradation [of man] can be only a penalty, and as every penalty presupposes a crime, reason alone is forced to accept original sin." He asserted that "our fatal inclination to evil" is a truth attested by every age, "and since this inclination is always more or less victorious over conscience and laws, man has never been able to recognize and deplore this sorry condition." It is his condition nonetheless. Man finds "he cannot be wicked without being evil, nor evil without being degraded, nor degraded without being punished, nor punished without being

12. *The Saint Petersburg Dialogues,* Jack Lively, *The Works of Joseph de Maistre,* 254, 252, 194, 188.

guilty." Maistre further declared that "nothing is so well attested, nothing so universally accepted under one form or another, nothing finally so intrinsically plausible as the theory of original sin."[13]

Such was the religious belief—rigorous, somber, pessimistic—of Joseph de Maistre. Not that his faith did not have its sweeter side, complete with solace and joy and meaning, but admittedly the prevailing tenor was one of duty and authority, moral sobriety and self-denial. Having examined said belief from a number of angles, both here and in earlier pages, it is now time to turn to the stated subject of this chapter, namely, Maistre's defense of Catholicism and his highly critical view of Protestantism. It will be seen that his position on this subject closely parallels that of René Guénon.

Though each demonstrated wide sympathies within the traditional religious sphere—Maistre's toward the higher paganisms of antiquity as well as his own Catholicism, and Guénon's toward all orthodox religious forms—neither could muster much sympathy toward their junior partners in the western branch of Christianity. (At first sight this seems more understandable in the case of Maistre, who remained loyal to Catholicism throughout his life and thus logically opposed to Protestantism, whereas Guénon—as observed earlier—abandoned his ancestral faith in favor of Islam, a detail that raises questions more profitably addressed elsewhere.)

In Maistre's view, Christianity was the world's uniquely, divinely revealed religion, and Catholicism its only genuine form. He believed the religion of Christ to be a law of love, yet gave precedence to the authority of the teaching church over the teaching itself. "If it were permitted," he wrote in "Lettre a une dame russe..." ("Letter to a Russian Lady"), "to establish degrees of importance among things of divine institution, I would place the hierarchy before dogma, since it is indispensable to the maintenance of the faith."[14] Ecclesiastical authority, then, must be respected and obeyed, a principle greatly diminished by Protestantism, he charged, and also little recognized by the many forms of illuminism then in vogue. Despite Maistre's affection for illuminism, he admitted its aversion to sacer-

13. Ibid., 200.
14. *Throne and Altar*, 134.

dotal hierarchy, a stance he believed incompatible with Catholic social order.

Owing to his emphasis on authority, Maistre went so far as to say that Christianity rested entirely on the Sovereign Pontiff. Without the office of the Pontiff, he wrote in *Du Pape*, the entire structure of Christianity "is mined, and awaits no more than the development of certain circumstances . . . to crumble entirely."[15] Unlike the arrangements in other Christian polities, papal authority formed the very essence of Catholicism, and the Pontiff's rights and supremacy were absolutely sacred. Protestants "call us papists," Maistre said, "and they are entirely right on the word; they deceive themselves . . . only in the signification they give it."[16]

Predictably, Maistre was a strong supporter not only of papal authority but of papal infallibility, as made especially clear in *Du Pape*, where he declared that infallibility in the spiritual order and sovereignty in the temporal order "are two perfectly synonymous words. They both express that great power which dominates all powers, from which all powers are derived, which governs and is not governed, which judges and is not judged."[17] Maistre moderated his view somewhat by distinguishing between the authority of secular sovereignty and the infallibility of the papacy. In doing so he noted that "infallibility is humanly supposed in the one case and divinely promised in the other." He refrained from using the arguments of those who had considered infallibility "under the theological point of view."[18] According to Richard Lebrun, he sought rather to employ his own unusual apologetic method[19] to convince Gallican readers of the logical necessity of recognizing papal infallibility. Assuming these readers believed in the Church's divinely ordained teaching, and that they (Frenchmen in this case) likewise understood the concept of secular sovereignty, he hoped to lead them by analogy to foreswear their Gallicanism in favor of the ultramontane

15. Ibid.
16. Citing "Lettre sur le Christianisme," in *Throne and Altar*, 135.
17. Ibid.
18. Ibid.
19. Ibid., 135–36, wherein Maistre argues "that theological truths are only general truths, manifested and divinized in the religious sphere."

position. Maistre insisted that "the Sovereign Pontiff speaking freely, and, as the scholastics say, ex cathedra, has never erred and will never err on faith."[20]

In the discussion of papal infallibility, Maistre cited a bit of traditional knowledge (to wit, the view that holds there is in man a division between soul and spirit) to illustrate the manner in which he would affirm a doctrine unless and until it fell victim to the pontiff's infallible ruling. He would affirm it, he said, unless "I am warned that I am mistaken by the sole power which has a legitimate authority over human belief. In that case, I will not hesitate an instant. Whereas at the moment I have only the certitude of being right, I would then have the faith to be wrong." If, he said, he did not acquiesce to the pope's decree he would betray the principles that had dictated all of the work he had published thus far.[21]

But we digress. Let us return to the main point, which is this: How did Maistre view Protestantism? Given his public and private convictions, from both a Catholic and more broadly Christian perspective, how did he evaluate this newer form of Christianity that had arisen to challenge the Catholic Church? In a word: scathingly. In one of many diatribes against non-Catholics, he asked, in *Du Pape*: "What is a Protestant? He is a man who protests. Now what does it matter whether he protests one or several dogmas, against this one or against that one? He may be more or less protestant, but

20. Ibid. Gallicanism held that state authority and national customs overrule the Catholic Church at many points. Ultramontanism emphasized the pope's powers and prerogatives in civil government and temporal affairs.

21. Ibid., 136. The view in question, that man has both a soul and a spirit, had long been held by esotericists of various kinds and by Christians of various persuasions. That it piques the interest of both is not surprising, for it has ramifications both theoretical and practical, metaphysical and devotional. It has been denied by many Catholics and Protestants alike, especially in the modern era, despite Biblical verses such as 1 Thessalonians 5:23, 1 Corinthians 15:44, Hebrews 4:12, and others. That Maistre held to it, indeed, that he had encountered it in the first place, testifies to his wide reading and reflection in both esoteric and theological literature. It is a theory often ignored by theologians of different stripes, be they conservative or liberal. It is frequently dismissed as of little importance even when recognized as a question demanding at least some attention. To the contrary, we believe it is of considerable importance.

always he protests."[22] And to protest was to question established teaching authority and thus the teaching itself. It was "rebellion," a terrible crime in Maistre's eyes. Protestantism, then, was the great enemy of Europe, "the fatal ulcer." It was that which attached itself to sovereign bodies and consumed them. It was "the son of pride, the father of anarchy, the universal dissolvent." It was the "insurrection" of individual reason against general reason, the enemy of beliefs held in common by human societies.[23]

To Maistre, Protestantism was not only a religious heresy but a civil heresy, in that it freed people from "the yoke of obedience" and accorded them sovereignty, religious and otherwise. It thereby set pride against authority and put discussion in place of obedience. Church and state were affected equally, with Protestantism dominating the one sphere and "the rights of man" the other. "These two brothers have broken sovereignty in order to distribute it to the multitude."[24]

According to Richard Lebrun, it is significant that the principle of private judgment was the only Protestant principle of note to which Maistre devoted significant attention. This is not totally surprising, inasmuch as private judgment allowed questioning of authoritative teaching, and Maistre was always about defending just this. It is, however, worth noting that neither Martin Luther nor John Calvin held the view in so expansive a way as did some later Protestants. To be sure, the magisterial reformers rejected on scriptural grounds certain of the doctrines held by Rome, but they were adamant in holding their own doctrines to be authoritative. The issue in dispute, then, was not authority per se but whose authority. In the years that followed, however, private judgment—or the misunderstanding or abuse of private judgment—held increasing sway in Protestant lands, with the multiplication of sects a not surprising outcome. The splintering of Protestantism presented an irresistible target to Maistre, given his abiding interest in authority and its necessary conditions and the likely outcome if authority was undermined.

22. Ibid., 138.
23. Ibid., 138–39.
24. Ibid., 139.

In his apologia for Catholicism, then, Maistre stressed the issue of authority while ignoring completely the dispute that led Luther in the first place to deny the authority of the church and instead rely on his own interpretations of the Bible. There is in Maistre nary a word regarding the great theological questions of the sixteenth century: justification by faith, the place of good works, or free will and predestination. For Maistre, the issue of authority trumped them all and thus governed his tactical approach.

Granted the foregoing, a subconscious and therefore hidden motive may have been at work in Maistre's neglect of important theological questions. That possible motive is located in the striking similarity between Maistre's theology and that of the reformers themselves, an awkward circumstance that would have been troubling to Maistre if faced head-on. Is there not, ironically, an echo in Maistre of Luther's profound sense of the majesty and sovereignty of God, his emphasis on original sin and man's sinfulness, and—a key point here—his teaching on submission to secular authority. And what of Calvin? Does not the French reformer's teaching on predestination (a view also held by Luther) harmonize more or less with Maistre's emphasis on God's providential ordering of history? "With both Maistre and the reformers," Richard Lebrun observes, "there was an extreme emphasis on divine activity at the expense of human initiative."[25]

Then again, Maistre may have regarded discussion of the sixteenth century questions cited above—not counting those related to authority—as irrelevant to the eighteenth and nineteenth century religious landscape. After all, he believed the Protestant churches of his own day had moved well past them and deteriorated into varieties of Socinianism (a system of liberal and unitarian teachings), an exaggeration containing a measure of truth. In an 1814 letter to the Count de Bray, he blamed the doctrine of Sola Scriptura for its role in Protestantism's decline. It was, he wrote, easy to see that in recognizing only the authority of the Bible, while being subordinate to no interpretative authority beyond it, one would undercut all dogmas one after the other. There was not, therefore, a point of Christian

25. Ibid., 140.

belief "that Protestantism has not attacked and destroyed in the mind of its partisans. . . . This unfortunate system has allied itself with philosophism, the second owing the first its most dangerous weapons. And these two enemies of all belief have exercised on Europe so fatal an influence that one exaggerates little in saying that this fair part of the world has no more religion."[26] Perhaps Maistre should be forgiven such a broad, un-nuanced declaration, since much of his world had been de-Christianized, owing to the French Revolution and its Napoleonic extension.

Despite the periodic waxing and waning of the churches over the next century, by the time of René Guénon, religious belief in much of Europe appeared indeed to be following a steadily downward trajectory. Not surprisingly, in Guénon's analysis as in Maistre's, much of the initial blame rested with Protestantism. So here, too, our traditionally-minded duo were thinking along the same lines, finding in Protestantism the loci of many of the disintegrating forces of modernism. Their critique was not totally original but it was trenchant and insightful, stepping on many a progressive toe as it explored the decline of traditional faith.

According to Guénon, whose approach differed somewhat from his predecessor's owing in part to the elapse of a century with its consequent changes and developments, the "innumerable sects" and churches that had sprung from the Reformation were often characterized by a reduction of the doctrinal element "in the interests of the moral or sentimental element," a phenomenon reflecting a "general diminishing of intellectuality." It was no mere happenstance, Guénon declared, that the Reformation had coincided chronologically with the Renaissance, that is, with the beginning of the modern period in thought, art, and technology. Owing to this chronological alignment, he said, the Protestant churches and smaller sectarian bodies were the only religious forms that were specifically modern, Catholicism and Orthodoxy having originated in antiquity and developed in the medieval period.[27]

---

26. Ibid., 141.
27. *East and West* (Ghent, NY: Sophia Perennis, 2001), 62.

Thus convinced that Protestantism's doctrinal element and intellectuality were much reduced, and that its worship was largely desacralized, Guénon confidently identified certain branches of Protestantism as "pseudo-religion," resembling more a type of philosophical conviction than an expression of true religion. He applied the same term to the many neo-spiritualist sects that had sprung up in Protestant countries, charging they were rooted in the same tendencies and state of mind as "liberal Protestantism." "The place of religion," he said, "owing to the suppression of the intellectual element . . . is taken by religiosity, or, in other words, by a mere sentimental aspiration, more or less vague and inconsistent; and this religiosity is to religion just about what the shadow is to the body." He further accused modernism of attempting to introduce its "mentality" into Catholicism itself, "an attempt that has broken against the force of the traditional outlook, whose sole refuge, in the modern West, appears to be Catholicism."[28] The limited success of modernist infiltration he had observed was to gain momentum over the following decades, thus partially undermining Catholicism's self-identity as a bulwark against modernist influences.

At first glance, Guénon and Maistre appear equally intransigent in their unfavorable view of Protestantism. Yet Maistre expressed an occasional moderating statement, some on a personal note and others of a more doctrinal and political nature. Despite his generally low estimate of the non-Roman churches, Maistre regarded himself—somewhat credulously—as unprejudiced in the matter. Among men of a convinced position, he claimed in a letter to the Count de Bray, "it would be difficult to find one more free of prejudices than I. I have a great many friends among the Protestants; and now that their system is crumbling they become more dear to me."[29] During his years in Switzerland and Russia, he formed enduring friendships with Protestants and Orthodox alike and expressed great interest in the prospect of Christian reunion.

Yet from what quarter would it come? Always the Anglophile, Maistre saw in the Church of England a possible partner in reunit-

---

28. Ibid., 62–63.
29. *Throne and Altar*, 141.

ing the churches. In *Considerations on France*, he observed that revolutionary tyranny had chased thousands of French priests from their homeland, thereafter in many cases to live in exile among Protestant peoples. This crime of the revolutionaries, he said, had become an instrument of Providence, and subsequent relations between French clergy, especially bishops, and non-Catholics helped dispel many of the hatreds and prejudices that had hitherto obtained. The considerable emigration of French clergy to England appeared to Maistre an event of capital importance. "Surely," he said, "words of peace will have been spoken and projects for reconciliation formed during this extraordinary meeting. Even if mutual hopes are all that result, this would be a lot."[30]

If Christians were to be reconciled, then, Maistre looked toward England. Presbyterianism, in which he included the Calvinism of the French, was unsuitable for the purpose. "Presbyterianism," he declared, "was a French, and consequently an exaggerated, creation; there are no means of getting to know one another." By contrast, the Church of England, containing both Catholic and Protestant elements, could play a mediating role, communicating between Rome on the one hand and the remote and "too-insubstantial religion" of Calvinism on the other. Thus the Church of England could serve "as one of those chemical intermediates capable of combining otherwise incompatible elements."[31]

For all of his criticism of non-Catholic Christianity, Maistre's longing for reunion was clearly a genuine impulse. It was revealing not only of his sense of mission but of his personal nature, which was at heart that of a kind and charitable man, despite the sometimes disturbing images that appear in his writings. In the 1780s he saw Freemasonry as the vehicle for reunion; later it was the Church of England. It was the vision of a man who was something of a mediating figure himself. Despite his not unjustified image as an unbending Ultramontane defender of Catholic authority, he was in his writings generally happy to appeal to the heretical Origen of Alexandria, to work the themes of Christian Platonism (by way of

30. *Considerations on France,* 19.
31. Ibid., 19

the Protestant philosopher Ralph Cudworth, among others), and to draw inspiration from Masonry and other esoteric currents. Even more, this defender of throne and altar allowed for salvation outside the church, not because of any dogmatic laxity on his part but because of his faith in God's justice. Hence even a man who believed himself in good faith "in the way of truth although he is really in that of error" will be judged by a just God. It is very strange, then, he wrote, "that we have such fear that God does not know to render justice to every one."[32]

32. In "Lettre a une dame protestante" ("Letter to a Protestant Lady"), cited in *Throne and Altar*, 153.

6

Joseph de Maistre
and America

AMERICAN READERS might be forgiven for asking: Why are Joseph
de Maistre's life and doctrine relevant to their own lives and beliefs
in the twenty-first century? After all, what does a long-deceased
monarchist, ultramontane Catholic, Old World diplomat and jurist,
and doubter of Enlightenment (and, by implication, its progressive
reverberations down through the years) have to do with a dynamic,
post-modern, and technologically proficient republic, complete
with informal empire and sharply divided populace?

Quite a bit actually, or so it seems to us. Maistre's greatest gift to
American readers, and to anyone else who might choose to read
him, is principally located in his unwavering mission to face and
answer the hard questions concerning human nature, religion, and
metaphysics, and, secondarily, to apply his answers to social and
political theory. Hence his political differences with the American
polity do not end his usefulness to the American public, but rather
stimulate a critical look at the strengths and weaknesses of the
American system even as they instruct in the foundational issues of
human nature and the human predicament more broadly. Moreover, in that he situates human nature and the human predicament
in an overarching transcendental schema, he provides an alternative
to American tendencies to philosophize horizontally, à la more
recent figures from William James and John Dewey to John Rawls
and Richard Rorty.

Not surprisingly, Maistre fixed blame on the American Revolution
for inspiring the French Revolution, the latter a "satanic" epoch in
Maistre's eyes, and thus a point of evidence against the nefarious
nature of its predecessor. There were, however, Europeans who

believed otherwise. In Britain, Edmund Burke—who would later excoriate the French Revolution and its perpetrators—sympathized with the colonists, extending an olive branch and speaking before Parliament on behalf of American grievances. Others, in the wake of America's subsequent victory, thought the American experiment a workable model for republican government in France and elsewhere. Yet Maistre would have none of it. Even if the American republic succeeded over time—and he was doubtful it would—he thought success would be the product of unique circumstances, an exception by virtue of long held English traditions of representative government and common law, as opposed to the influence of the abstract theories of the *philosophes* and other Enlightenment sources.

That the two revolutions were different in many ways was a view Maistre gladly allowed, for it bolstered his general argument against republicanism wherever else it might raise its head. As he and others could plainly see, America's British heritage was a defining difference, as this had grounded the revolution and nascent republic in deeply rooted, practical principles instead of utopian visions. Among those principles was, of course, "No taxation without representation." Contrary to popular views, the rebellion was not set in motion by the price of tea or any particular tax but, rather, over whether the British Crown and Parliament could tax Americans in the first place—as they had recently been doing—without the consent of colonial assemblies. The colonists were concerned whether, by giving way on the Tea Act, they would set a precedent by which the British government might be emboldened to govern the colonies directly in ways it had never done before. Americans were accustomed to the long-established chartered right of governing themselves, hence initially it was not the colonists but George III who intended to enact revolutionary changes by increasing royal prerogatives.

According to historian Russell Kirk, the patriot contention "closely resembled the argument of the English Whigs against the policies of James II—the protest that had triumphed in the Glorious Revolution of 1688."[1] Thus the patriot leaders (despite a minor-

---

1. *The Roots of American Order* (La Salle, IL: Open Court Publishing, 1975), 395.

Joseph de Maistre and America

ity of radical dissidents mostly below the surface) went to war largely to preserve established political usage and not to foment modification of the social structure. It was less a revolution than a War of Independence.

This was of course far different than the French Revolution, which instead of attempting to reform and preserve the old order was, in Edmund Burke's words, "a revolution of theoretic dogma."[2] The radical and abstract doctrines of Rousseau and Condorcet, Turgot and Thomas Paine held the field, defying history and breaking with the past, and thus enabling the promethean attempt to transform human society and even human nature into something they could never be. According to an astute European observer, the American war "was a defensive revolution" and thus "of course finished, at the moment when it had overcome the attack, by which it had been occasioned." The events in France, however, were "true to the character of a most violent revolution, [and] could not but proceed as long as there remained objects for it to attack, and it retained strength for the assault." The same commentator allowed that the American war was not unsullied by persecutions, cruelties, confiscations, and the exiling of honest persons, yet these were incidental byproducts. "[W]hat are all these single instances of injustice and oppression," he asked, "compared with the universal flood of misery and ruin, which the French revolution let loose upon France, and all the neighbouring countries? . . . [N]ever, as in France, was the contempt of all rights, and of the very simplest precepts of humanity, made the general maxim of legislation, and the unqualified prescription of systematic tyranny."[3]

As we have seen, Maistre could hardly help being relatively moderate in his comments regarding the American Revolution, owing to the character of that conflict. He could not help remarking, despite his generally hostile view toward republicanism, on the differences between the purposes and trajectories of the American and French

2. Kirk, *The Roots of American Order*, 396.
3. Ibid., 398, 399–400. Comments are by Friedrich Gentz, publicist and statesman of Prussian origin who first translated Edmund Burke's *Reflections on the French Revolution* into German.

81

revolutions. Yet his views on monarchy and social stability remained quite unmoved. He was convinced, as intimated above, that the American experiment would only succeed owing to causes that could not be replicated elsewhere, for it stood as an anomaly in the history of nations. Nor was he impressed by its Constitution and Bill of Rights; his trust was in the wisdom of the ages, a wisdom less easily perceived by purveyors of the newer statecraft but—he believed—of more bedrock value in the long run. Nor did he mention by name the great men of America's founding, or the enduring insights of *The Federalist Papers*. Despite his belief in the importance of eminent politicians in building durable polities, one finds no praise for Washington or Franklin, Adams or Jefferson. Even the presence of Freemasons among the founders did not soften his views. Either he was largely unaware of the fact, or he assumed his own mystical brand of Masonry did not obtain among the Americans.[4]

If Maistre had wished to single out one of the founding fathers for special criticism—though he did not deign to do so—he could not have chosen better than Thomas Jefferson, who was indeed excessive in some of his pronouncements. One need not wonder what Maistre would have thought of Jefferson's universal vision of an ever-spreading, self-governing republicanism to be achieved—as he wrote to John Adams in 1823—at the expense of great violence and suffering. "[R]ivers of blood must yet flow, & years of desolation pass over," Jefferson declared (and this, at the age of eighty), "yet the object is worth rivers of blood, and years of desolation." Though acutely aware of the sins and errors of various monarchs, Maistre never wavered in his belief that throne and altar—and the stability they provided—remained infinitely better than periodic revolutionary blood-lettings in the interests of democracy and self-rule. He would have been equally appalled at the sentiment expressed in another of Jefferson's letters, written from Paris to William Smith in 1787, which declared that "The tree of liberty must be refreshed from time to time with the blood of patriots and tyrants." In the person of

---

4. Nine of the fifty-six signers of the Declaration of Independence were Masons; thirteen of the thirty-nine delegates who ratified the Constitution were Masons.

Jefferson, then, patrician and statesman though he was, Maistre would have discerned the archetypal face of democracy, arguably a figure more radical by half than America's other major founders.

To the extent the founders relied on the views of John Locke,[5] to that extent Maistre was even further alienated from them. In the *Soirées*, he engaged in a lengthy critique of the English philosopher, insisting on his mediocrity and challenging his views on the origin of ideas. "Locke is perhaps the only author known," Maistre suggested [in the words of the Count, his mouthpiece], "who has taken the trouble to refute his whole book or to declare it useless, from the beginning, by telling us *that all our ideas come from the senses or from reflection.*" Locke was brazen enough, Maistre said, "to hold *that a single atheist* in the world was for him a sufficient justification for denying *that the idea of God is innate in man,* or, to put this another way [and this was Maistre's clincher], that a single deformed child, born, for example, without eyes, would prove that sight is not natural to man." By his rejection of innate ideas, Maistre believed, Locke undercut his own position and damaged the moral sense by removing its true foundation. In Maistre's opinion, if an idea did not preexist, the senses could never give birth to it. As we have seen, this view was axiomatic to him. As he put it: "Every rational belief is founded on antecedent knowledge, for man can learn nothing except because he knows. Since syllogism and induction always start from already known principles, it must be admitted that before reaching a particular truth we must already know it in part."[6] He also dismissed Locke's theories regarding social contract, individualism, and anti-monarchism.

---

5. Kirk, *The Roots of American Order*, 292. Locke was but one of a number of influences on the founders. Jefferson praised him highly but more frequently cited such juridical authorities as Sir Edward Coke and Lord Kames. John Adams, the most learned of the Federalists, cited Locke favorably but relatively seldom. He was commended as but one of several English friends of liberty, among them Sir Philip Sidney, James Harrington, John Milton, Henry Neville, Gilbert Burnet, and Benjamin Hoadly.

6. *The Saint Petersburg Dialogues*, in *The Works of Joseph de Maistre*, trans. Jack Lively, 239–42.

Despite Maistre's criticisms, early America had its conservative public figures, with Alexander Hamilton and members of the Federalist Party the leading examples. Of course, the loyalists during the Revolution had been conservatives after a fashion, but conservatives in the manner of Whigs loyal to king and parliament. Thus they held to a more self-interested and temperamental conservatism than to a bold proclamation of traditional thought and sentiment. With the loyalist side having been defeated in the war, it was left to Hamilton and the Federalists to fill the conservative vacuum. This they attempted to do. Though devoted to liberty, they promoted a strong union, believed men were essentially unequal (in natural endowment), believed *vox populi* (voice of the people) was seldom *vox Dei* (the voice of God), and promoted commercial interests and a national bank. It was left to the Jeffersonian Republicans, the more egalitarian party, to represent poor farmers and the working class and to oppose strengthening the federal government. Needless to say, neither party would ever be acceptable to Maistre.

Yet despite his criticisms of the American republic (not to mention the French republic), Maistre was far from favoring an unmediated top-down form of government as an alternative. Of course, that he did so has been the view of his critics, whether those of standing such as the Marxist Harold Laski or the liberal Isaiah Berlin, or the many lesser commentators given to repeating the customary line. In fact, to the contrary, Maistre maintained views of a moderate and balanced nature. Though considerably distant from American principles they were certainly not far from British principles. According to political scientist Cara Camcastle, Maistre preferred a "tempered monarchy" rather than anything approaching a proto-totalitarian state. Citing his *Study on Sovereignty,* she notes he believed that political subjects had the right, by means of certain bodies—councils or assemblies variously composed—to inform the king "of their needs, to denounce abuses, and legally to pass their grievances and their very humble remonstrances to him." In such a system, the king was expected to observe the laws of the nation's constitution, just as other citizens were expected to do. In addition, the king was required "to heed the judgments of other bodies ... such as the hereditary magistrates in the *parlements* not appointed by the king."[7] Hence countervailing forces provided checks and balances, a principle well known to the constitution-makers of America.

The Savoyard's cautions and criticisms eventually won a modest audience in the American republic. The Catholic convert Orestes Brownson, New England intellectual and publicist, led the American discovery of Maistre in the 1840s. Partial to Maistre's conviction that constitutions "are generated, not made," he relied on Maistre's views as a source of his polemics against what he considered the excesses of American democracy. Thus by the mid-nineteenth century, it seems, America "was self-assured enough for Brownson to cite Maistre's writings as a remedy to rampant individualism."[8] Yet Brownson's favorable opinion, uttered in the wake of a bumptious Jacksonian democracy, enlisted but little support for either Maistre or his writings.

Although Maistre ignored political figures in his writings on America, he was not ignored in turn, at least by one of them, one who happened to be the son of a president and a future president himself, John Quincy Adams. From 1809 to 1814, Adams was American ambassador to Russia, his years in St. Petersburg partially overlapping Maistre's. Maistre cultivated the American's friendship, and Adams's memoirs contain a number of references to the Sardinian ambassador.

When Adams first met Maistre in November 1809, he found in him "a man of sense and vivacity in conversation." At a diplomatic dinner in May 1810, he sat next to Maistre and discussed the "Slavonian language" with him. Considerably later, Maistre lent him a manuscript copy of his translation of Plutarch's treatise on the delays of divine justice and a work by the seventeenth century Jesuit theologian, Denis Petau. In March 1814, on returning the Petau and other books, Adams recorded his final impressions of Maistre, which are worth quoting in full:

---

7. Cara Camcastle, review of *Joseph de Maistre's Life, Thought, and Influence: Selected Studies*, ed. Richard Lebrun (Montreal-Kingston: McGill-Queen's University Press, 2001), www.firstprinciplesjournal.com (Spring 2006).

8. Joseph Eaton, "'This babe-in-arms': Joseph de Maistre's critique of America," in *Joseph de Maistre and the Legacy of Enlightenment*, 42.

The Count is a religious man, a Roman Catholic, with all the prejudices of his sect. He is a great admirer of Malebranche, and has Locke and Condillac in horror. He thinks it a very sublime idea of Malebranche's, that God is the *place* in which spirits exist, as space is the place of bodies. So differently are the minds of men constituted, that this comparison conveys to my understanding no idea at all. It rather detracts from the idea I have of the Deity, because it takes away its most essential characteristic, *intelligence*. It draws closely to the absurdities of the Greek philosophers, who thought water, air, fire, and what not, God. The Count was particularly harsh upon Locke for his doctrine that we have no innate ideas. He insists that all our ideas are innate, and that a child can never learn anything but what he knows already. He expressed a mean opinion of Locke's genius, and said he was the origin of all the materialism of the eighteenth century; that Condillac was the corrupter of France; that Kant, the German metaphysician, though an atheist himself, had gone far to demolish Locke's pretence that experience was the source of our ideas; and that there is now wanting only a *coup de pied* to demolish such fellows as Locke and Condillac altogether.[9]

Here the erudite Adams shows himself a keen observer of men and ideas, revealing as he does a Maistre clearly recognizable as both a personality and a thinker. In this relationship we find at least an instance, despite the disagreements cited above, where Old World and New were as one in the civilized life of the mind.

Maistre's pessimistic view of the American experiment, rendered early in the nation's history and in the heated context of what had taken place during the revolution in France, is understandable. No one could have expected a different assessment from him, given his throne and altar convictions and his opposition to republican government and written constitutions. Does his assessment of nascent America—then and now—ring true? Maistre wrote his criticisms at the beginning of the nation's history; we have the advantage of two centuries and more to make an evaluation. He saw America as a liberal experiment rooted in rebellion but tempered by British heritage; we know it to be an enduring and largely successful enterprise

9. Richard Lebrun, *Joseph de Maistre: An Intellectual Militant*, note 49, 316–17.

replete with wealth, power, resilience, personal liberty—not to mention a host of seemingly intractable problems internally and externally, not a few of them of its own making. Maistre would still identify many faults to catalogue; American conservatives and traditionalists do, too.

If American history is the unfolding of a liberal experiment in governance and social development, one might ask where that leaves non-liberals. Is there a place for them? In a liberal republic—if that is a fair designation of the American polity—what does a conservative wish to conserve?

In the middle of the past century, the American literary critic Lionel Trilling famously declared, in the preface to his *The Liberal Imagination*, that liberalism was in his time not only the dominant but the sole intellectual tradition in America. Many have agreed with him, some with pride and some with regret. Trilling did not deny there were impulses toward conservatism or reaction but held that they did not constitute a coherent intellectual doctrine (excepting some rather marginal and isolated ecclesiastical positions); rather, they found expression in action or as "irritable mental gestures which seek to resemble ideas."

If there is a conservative intellectual enclave amidst this reputed liberal hegemony, it is something quite apart from Maistre's throne and altar version of the concept. Yet it is also something more than the preservation of personal freedom as espoused by many self-identified conservatives. One cannot reduce the essence of conservatism to the right to do as one pleases provided one does not infringe on the similar rights of others, useful as that formulation may be. The essence of the American heritage, conservatively speaking, would seem to be located in its recognized authorities—something to which Maistre might resonate—without which no people can perpetuate a cohesive and functioning polity. Personal freedom, personal rights, are understandably cherished, but authority—based on the legitimacy of federal, state, and local governments—is the foundation of political life, even as customs, habits, shared values, and voluntary associations are the foundations of social life.

American authority was established by the founding generation. Though the Fathers had rebelled against a lawful government;

though their ideas reflected a measure of deism, Whiggery, and Lockean theory; though they spoke much of equality in somewhat ambiguous language, what they left in the founding documents was a prescription for the manner in which their descendants would govern themselves. There was no monarch, there was no pope, but there was law, there was government, there was authority.

However much the Fathers leavened their British heritage and common sense instincts with Enlightenment novelties, they belatedly ratified a Constitution and Bill of Rights that spelled out the necessary workings of the polity; that prescribed the areas in which government could legitimately limit the rights of individual citizens, and that yet protected the reasonable rights thereof. The development of a judicial tradition added to the sense of restraint embedded in the founding documents by assuring (ideally) that the nation's laws did not reflect only the will of the moment but rather a tradition that had been developed and refined over centuries.

The fact that the Founders have been venerated as "Fathers" indicates a further element of conservative tendency. It has a note of piety in it, of deep respect for the men who gave the nation its identity and legitimacy. It echoes also a respect for parental figures in general, for ancestors whose wisdom and sacrifices made possible the very existence of an independent polity.

In opposition to the displaced Royalists of France, Maistre himself argued that history could never be repealed, that the Revolution with all of its atrocities and excesses and alterations could never be erased or covered over. France was no longer the nation of an earlier era and never would be so again. Instead, the dynamics of the Revolution—a purging and redeeming force—had created a much modified state of affairs, a new political and social reality that needed to be assimilated rather than crushed by the Restoration. Historical lessons had to be read, marked, studied, and inwardly digested. It was not enough to turn back the clock. It was a matter of moving forward while letting time heal the wounds from the national trauma, and of plucking a few embers from wisdom's dying fire to help illuminate the path.

So, too, Americans of a traditionalist bent cannot repeal history. In a Maistrian vein, they may be most effective by accepting and assimilating the American experiment root and branch, by celebrating the good and decrying the bad; by, as it were, cultivating its wheat and blighting its tares. Yet tares will remain, even until the last day. Progressive energumens never rest. Bereft of the Absolute, they strive incessantly for that which can never be had, even as they corrupt and destroy that which is. The conservative, the traditionalist, is freed from such secular manias to one degree or another, yet humbled by the knowledge that he is not above temptation himself. Always he must beware when he stands, lest he fall. He can be thankful that he has an enduring heritage; a nation of traditions despite its untraditional origins.

Though a young nation, America is the oldest living republic with the oldest written constitution, the oldest democracy, and the oldest federal system. Unlike other nations, it lacks a constitution risen from the mists of time but instead knows when and where and why its own constitution was hammered out and what it has meant in its history. The nation was founded in violence and idealism; its roots drew from soils both tainted and pure; its founders were fallible and fallen human beings. But they bequeathed to their posterity a legitimacy that has survived many a trial. As Maistre observed, the American experiment based itself largely on British heritage, thereby linking itself to a past older and a tradition deeper than its own. This organic attachment to a Mother Country has served it well.

Life in the sublunary world is always messy, divided, incomplete. No one had a sharper eye than Maistre for the ironies and absurdities and tragedies of life, nor for its mysteries and compensations. What would be his assessment if he could see America today? Ever the realist, he would see it warts and all, and perhaps recognize benignly its unique contribution to a less than perfect world.

7

Tradition and Modernity

If Joseph de Maistre had distilled his views on tradition, both metaphysical and political, into a single concise volume, he would have written something very much like René Guénon's *Spiritual Authority and Temporal Power*.[1] True to form, Guénon presented his own views on the subject in highly organized fashion, expounding in principle and detail the attributes of the traditional spiritual and temporal domains and the relations between them. Drawing examples from both India and the medieval West, he presented his thesis that in a healthy traditional civilization knowledge is supreme over action and the sacerdotal class over the royal class.

So coherent and complete is Guénon's presentation that we find it expedient to consider his work on the subject before turning back to Maistre's presentation. In doing so, we depart from our practice of considering Maistre first, which we have done until now owing to his position as the principal figure of our work. Here we shall allow Guénon to build the framework of the discussion.

In keeping with his custom, Guénon makes clear from the beginning of *Spiritual Authority and Temporal Power* that he does not wish to engage contemporary political questions or current events generally. Instead, he wishes to address the domain of principles. Even so, in his preface, he alludes to "incidents" that had drawn attention to the general questions he planned to treat, incidents involving a confrontation in 1926 between the right wing political movement, *Action Française*, and Pope Pius XI, who was soon to condemn the organization. By holding to a stress on principles, Guénon was able, he asserted, "to remain aloof from all those discussions, polemics, and quarrels of school or party in which we

---

1. *Spiritual Authority and Temporal Power* (Ghent, NY: Sophia Perennis, 2001).

have no wish to be involved, directly or indirectly, in any way or to any degree."[2]

Guénon further observed that his study transcends all particular forms of temporal power and even all forms of spiritual authority. Moreover, he said, it largely transcends even religion as such, for spiritual authority does not always or everywhere assume a religious form as it does in the West. He allows that this circumstance is difficult for Westerners to comprehend, accustomed as they are to view religion as the exclusive source of spiritual authority. Nevertheless, he speaks from the point of view of traditional metaphysics, that is, from the repository of immutable and essential principles beyond all contingencies. In his view, religion is something quite different from metaphysics. As a form of doctrine and practice, religion is subject to contingency; to decadence or renewal, to decline or expansion. Not that he finds religion a negligible factor. Anyone familiar with his writings knows that he considers the traditional religions both East and West to be vehicles of revealed truth. Moreover, he maintains that religion provides most people with what spiritual understanding and moral direction they possess, while metaphysics is reserved for a relative few.

According to Guénon, such evidence as we have indicates an opposition between the spiritual and the temporal powers throughout the ages of history and even long before historical times. He dates this opposition, or division, to the period of the "primordial tradition" itself, employing here his term for an archaic form of religion from which all later religions descended. The division between spiritual and temporal power is thus an integral element in human society, with spiritual power standing at the top of caste or class, temporal power on the next rung down, and the remaining classes in their respective places in the traditional hierarchy.

Regarding hierarchy, Guénon had no patience with anyone who advocated egalitarian schemes. Owing to the differing natures and capacities of human individuals, he believed a hierarchy of one kind or another is unavoidable; if not a traditional one then one based on later "deviations." Those who refuse to recognize the differences

2. Ibid., 2.

between individuals advocate a theory "contrary to all established facts and belied even by simple observation, since equality is really nowhere to be found."[3] Guénon pointed out that the words designating caste in India signify nothing more than "individual nature," indicating all the characteristics of a human individual that differentiate it from all other human individuals.[4]

In effect, Guénon says, each man is suited by nature to carry out certain functions to the exclusion of all others. Hence the caste system in India, not to mention analogous institutions elsewhere in both East and West, has specific rules by which individuals are assigned their place in the hierarchy. That such a model of social organization is less than perfect will be a surprise to no one, but invariably it has been the way in which traditional societies have chosen to arrange themselves. To this day, every society continues to sort its individual members in one way or another into professions or occupations suitable to their natures or abilities. Not only that, but the basic divisions in societies remain surprisingly constant, a subject to which we shall return.

Caste distinctions and corresponding differences in social function, Guénon asserts, are the result of a rupture of the primordial unity, a development that separated spiritual and temporal powers from one other. Yet despite the separation, he says, there remained a "perfect harmony" by which the original accord remained intact. Only at a later stage was this distinction to develop into opposition and rivalry, thus introducing conflict between the two powers and opening the way for "inferior functions"—or, rather, for the persons who embody them—to usurp supremacy over the higher ranks.

At this point, owing to its relevance regarding conflict between higher and lower powers, Guénon introduces the traditional Hindu doctrine of the four successive ages into which the history of humanity is divided. This doctrine, he observes, is found not only in India but among the ancient Greeks and Romans, also. "These four ages are the different phases humanity traverses," he says, "as it moves away from the principle and so away from primordial unity

3. Ibid., 8.
4. Ibid.

and spirituality." These ages, involving increased usurpation of power by ever more inferior members of the hierarchy, reflect a "progressive materialization" inherent in the development of the cycle of manifestation.[5] At present, he asserts, humanity finds itself in the last of these four ages, the *Kali-Yuga* or "dark age," a period ripe for large-scale subversion of the normal order of society.

In Hinduism, the first two castes—Brahmins and Kshatriyas—represent the spiritual and temporal powers, respectively. From a broader point of view, they serve as analogues of comparable powers in every civilization. In our era, late in the *Kali-Yuga* (which Guénon says began in the sixth century before the Christian era), the Kshatriyas attempt usurpation of Brahmin supremacy. In like manner, Vaishyas and Sudras, the lower ranks of the hierarchy, attempt usurpation as well. The result is social confusion and the overthrow of all hierarchy.

Even so, this does not mean spiritual and temporal powers (sacerdotal and royal powers, as they are traditionally called) lose all their appropriate functions. Rivalry is less about usurpation of *function* than about position within the social organism; that is, it is a struggle for supremacy within the hierarchy. For example, having been customarily subject to the spiritual authority, the Kshatriya warrior and governing class may revolt against it. If it succeeds, it declares itself independent of spiritual domination, going so far as to subordinate the spiritual authority to its own ends, thus reversing the traditional order. Henceforth, the temporal power occupies the rightful place of the Brahmins, who draw their authority not from sensible support but from invisible entities. For spiritual authority is "an entirely intellectual strength," Guénon explains, "whose name is 'wisdom' and whose only force is that of truth."[6] Not so the temporal authority, which exercises power in the material sense, in a strength and force that manifests visibly and outwardly.

Lest any confusion arise, Guénon tells in detail what he means when he speaks of sacerdotal and royal powers, that is, of priesthood and royalty within the hierarchy. As already indicated, the

5. Ibid., 10.
6. Ibid., 17.

royal function, the function of the Kshatriyas, includes all that can properly be called "government." The entire caste exercises governance, with the king (if the government is a monarchy) as the paramount figure. Serving both king and country, so to speak, is an array of administrative, judicial, and military officials. The mandate of the Kshatriyas is to maintain internal and external order; to protect against criminality within and aggression from without. Its symbolism in diverse traditions includes the scales and the sword, representing civil justice and military strength.

As regards the priesthood (the Brahmins in Hindu society), its essential function is to conserve and transmit traditional doctrine, in which all social organizations find their fundamental principles. As long as the traditions involved are authentically orthodox, that which is conserved and transmitted is considered immutable, impassible, and eternal. In the West, this function has taken a religious form, while in India it has not always done so. According to the *Rig-Veda*, the Brahmins speak as "Universal Man" from the mouth of *Purusha*—a cosmic being both immanent and transcendent. Whether explicitly religious or sacred in a non-religious form, the basic function of priesthood involves knowledge and teaching, and its proper attribute is wisdom.

Outward functions also belong to the priesthood, including performance of rites based on doctrinal knowledge. In the West, such accessory functions are generally seen as the principal and often the only responsibility of the priesthood, even though they are in fact secondary and contingent duties. This is because the "real nature" of the priesthood has been nearly forgotten, "this being one of the effects of the modern deviation, which negates all intellectuality."[7] As the depository and transmitter of traditional knowledge, Guénon explains, the priesthood communicates that knowledge to all who are capable of receiving it, according to intellectual capacity. Pure intellectuality, the knowledge of the principles, is reserved exclusively for the priesthood, whereas *applications* of traditional knowledge are developed by men whose functions place them in

---

7. Ibid., 19. By intellectuality, Guénon indicates pure intelligence and supra-formal knowledge.

proximity to the manifested world and its activities, and thus to persons to whom the applications apply.

Therefore the differences between the two highest orders in the hierarchy may be designated under the categories of "principles" and "applications," or divided between the metaphysical and physical domains. Deriving in turn from this distinction are the ancient mysteries of both East and West, between what were called the greater mysteries and the lesser mysteries, the former comprising knowledge of what is beyond nature and the latter knowledge of nature itself. According to Guénon, these in turn corresponded to the distinction between sacerdotal initiation and royal initiation. He observes that Dante, in the *De Monarchia*, declares that these two states lead to the Celestial Paradise and the Terrestrial Paradise, respectively. In the *Divine Comedy*, he observes, Dante asserts that the second serves only as a stage on the way to the first.

Aware that some may reproach him for using the word "caste" in discussing social organization, Guénon explains that the Indian terminology reflects more or less the functions found in every society, and thus its use is not unwarranted. Especially in the Middle Ages, he says, the West embodied a structure very much like the caste system, with the clergy corresponding to the Brahmins, the nobility to the Kshatriyas, the third-estate (merchants and craftsmen) to the Vaishyas, and the serfs to the Shudras. Though these were not castes in the full meaning of the term, the similarities are obvious enough. Guénon also observes that the Vaishyas, or what we would call the "bourgeoisie" or middle and upper middle classes, who accord a preponderant importance to economic considerations, are the dominant group in the modern West.

The Kshatriyas of traditional society—the class of warriors, nobles and government officials—receive their legitimacy through initiation by the only caste ranking above them, the Brahmins. Having received the guarantee of their power from the spiritual authority, they in turn use their power to ensure the Brahmins have the means to accomplish their functions of cultivating and then transmitting spiritual knowledge to the populace, peacefully sheltered from outside disturbances. Guénon points out that Hindu symbolism represents this relationship by the image of Skanda, lord of war,

Tradition and Modernity

protecting the meditation of Ganesha, lord of knowledge. He also notes that Hindu symbolism links these two gods by representing them as brothers, sons of Shiva, which in turn illustrates that spiritual and temporal powers proceed from a common principle. He further notes that a comparable relationship was taught in the Western Middle Ages, where Saint Thomas Aquinas declared that all human functions are subordinate to contemplation of the truth, and that those who govern civil life specifically serve the contemplatives.[8]

According to Guénon, temporal power brings about its own ruin when it disregards its subordination to and protection of the spiritual authority. This is so because everything belonging to the world of change, that is, to the world inhabited by Kshatriyas in India and warriors and nobles in the West, is itself subject to change. This caste or class, then, is not sufficient unto itself, for those living in the world of change only—that is, those living in the ebb and flow of the merely natural and human worlds without benefit of spiritual authority—are morally and metaphysically without reference to an immutable principle. Whenever the governing class usurps the place of the spiritual authority, then, it finds itself largely or entirely in the world of change or "becoming," a world with no immutable principles or finality to which it can anchor itself. It is the world of William James, that most American of philosophers, a man pleased with—or at least resigned to—an exclusively horizontal world recognizing no domain above or beyond itself. This is the world celebrated by the acolytes of progressive thought, by those who dominate public opinion in the West and urge the populace to embrace the never-ending struggle after the ever-receding goal; by those who reduce all life to the temporal, to succession, to process. The Kshatriya is at home in such a world, but he only thrives in it by subordinating himself to spiritual authority, which anoints him and teaches him wisdom.

Guénon finds an analogue of the "revolt of the Kshatriyas" in medieval Europe, especially in France from the time of Philip the Fair (1268–1314). Well before the rise of humanism in the Renaissance, Philip's jurists were busy reversing the order of the spiritual and temporal powers. Guénon thinks the start of the rupture was marked by the destruction of the Order of the Temple (or Knights Templar), an order which had served as a kind of link between East and West owing to its character as both a religious and martial—or spiritual and temporal—organization. Deeply in debt to the Templars, Philip tortured and executed many of their members on trumped up charges and pressured Pope Clement V to disband the order. By these actions, temporal power began to use spiritual authority for its own ends. Guénon says it is instructive that Dante attributed Philip's actions (which also included debasement of coinage) to "cupidity," the vice of greed, the vice not of a Kshatriya but of a Vaishya. "[W]e could say that when they enter a state of revolt, the Kshatriyas as it were degrade themselves, losing their own character and taking on that of a lower caste."[9]

From a political point of view, Guénon continues, modernity is inextricably linked to the national system that replaced the feudal system, a development that began in the fourteenth century with increasing centralization of power. In particular, the formation of the French nation was the work of its kings, who usurped the place of the spiritual authority and arrogated to themselves the role of final arbiter. Having seemingly realized its ambitions, the royal power only sowed the seeds of its ultimate demise, for the temporal realm, largely disconnected from spiritual authority, is one of untethered fluctuation, in which national entities—dispersed fragments of what was once Christendom—become ends in themselves and war against one another in ever more costly and destructive conflicts. If France, Guénon declares, was the first European country where monarchy was abolished (and the church persecuted) it was no accident, for France was the place where the nation state had started. The Revolution and its Napoleonic extension demonstrated the lengths to which the nationalist spirit—unstable, inconstant, mercurial as it is—can manifest itself in the wake of seizing power, first in devouring its own children and then in warring with its neighbors both defensively and offensively.

9. Ibid., 58.

Predictably, Guénon had acerbic things to say about Protestant countries where "national churches" had been established, in the course of which proper hierarchical relations had been reversed by subjugating the spiritual domain to the temporal. He traces the start of this subjugation to Martin Luther, who, he charges, was in political terms no more than an instrument of ambitious German princes.[10] Guénon was equally harsh in what he had to say about France, as alluded to above. In France, it was proponents of Gallicanism (the spirit of nationalism within the Roman Catholic Church) who sought to place temporal authority ahead of spiritual authority. This movement was one of a series of such efforts, wherein the secular power had, in the words of Joseph de Maistre, attempted "to rend the seamless robe" in favor of the monarchy.[11] As conceived by Louis XIV, Gallicanism sought to interpose itself in such a way as to make it seem that Rome continued to have priority, while true power resided in the monarch. If it had been successful, in Guénon's view, Gallicanism would have matched the achievement of the Anglican schism of Henry VIII, hitherto the most successful of such endeavors.

As noted at the start of the chapter, much of Guénon's thesis, rigorous and concise as it is, can be found in the work of Maistre, where it is located in multiple places but clearly recognizable in its similarity. Maistre believed that the Pope should be the final court of appeal in preventing abuses among the nations, thus placing spiritual authority over temporal authority. This, of course, agrees with Guénon's doctrine that the spiritual has precedent over the temporal (while agreeing also that the temporal power has legitimate authority in its own sphere). Spiritual supremacy is recognized owing to its infallible nature in matters of faith and morals, an argument Maistre was making a half century before Papal Infallibility was defined by the Vatican Council of 1870. Guénon was to hold the same view. "An authentic representative of a traditional

---

10. Needless to say, Luther was a devoutly religious man, a true wrestler with Christ, but political and military maneuvering did begin early on in areas of Protestant and Catholic tension.

11. *Spiritual Authority and Temporal Power*, 62.

doctrine," he says, "is necessarily infallible when he speaks in the name of this doctrine; and it must be clearly understood that this infallibility is attached, not to the individual, but to the function."[12]

Like Guénon, then, Maistre believed political authority should be subordinate to religious authority. Also like Guénon, he believed that spiritual and temporal authority were founded together and indissolubly linked (or, as Guénon put it, that Ganesha and Skanda are alike sons of Shiva). In Maistre's (and Guénon's) view, the origins of both spiritual and temporal authority are necessarily shrouded in mystery, a fact of capital importance. For, he says, obscure origins are the hallmark of legitimacy. Miracle, ritual, the favor of heaven; all are part and parcel of traditional order. Hence legendary or mythical beginnings, he insists, more adequately assure the wisdom of the governors and the consent of the governed than the shaky parliamentary systems and man-made constitutions of modern dreamers.

One can also find similarities between Maistre and Guénon in the patience they exhibit regarding the restoration of a traditional order in the wake of revolutionary (or evolutionary) change. Maistre embodied this quality by recommending against counterrevolution, if by this term is meant a revolution in reverse. In a notable expression, he declared his hope that "what they call the counterrevolution will be not a *contrary revolution* but the *contrary of revolution*";[13] not a shift from left-wing to right-wing violence but a passage from violence to order. Yet he believed there was no expeditious way to do this; no direct strategy available to reverse the attainments and debasements of the Revolution. He held this view not because of changes that had been made to the structure of the state only but rather because of changes to the political culture that had made such transformations possible. The old order in anything like its former glory was finished. The curtain that veiled the mysteries had been torn away. "The red bonnet," Maistre says, "in touching the royal forehead, made the traces of holy oil disappear . . . the charm

12. Ibid., 58.
13. Owen Bradley, *A Modern Maistre*, 220. Quotation from *Considerations on France*, OC 1:144–48.

was broken.... Lengthy profanations have destroyed the divine empire of national prejudices."[14]

All of this resonates with Guénon's view that hasty action is a mistake in attempts to reinstitute a traditional order. Never interested in practical political schemes, Guénon's point of view was that of spiritual realities, in the context of which he held that one can wait without anxiety as long as needed, for "this is the domain of the immutable and the eternal." Feverish attempts to restore traditional order, so characteristic of the modern world, prove that "our contemporaries really still hold to the temporal point of view even when they believe they have left it behind."[15] No matter how reduced authentic spiritual presence is in the modern world, Guénon asserted that its authority would always "prove the better part." For it contains that which is higher than purely human possibilities; weakened or dormant as it might be, it "still incarnates 'the one thing needful,' the only thing that does not pass away."[16]

14. Ibid., 224. Quotation from *Considerations*, OC 1:145.
15. *Spiritual Authority and Temporal Power*, 82.
16. Ibid., 83–84.

8

Maistre's
Relevance for Today

WE COME TO the end of our exposition and look now for major
themes and applications. The first allows us to review and reflect
upon Maistre's body of doctrine, upon his convictions and principles and ideas. The second invites us to explore the fund of possibilities inherent in his teaching. In our view, Maistre's ideas remain as
lively and provocative today as they were during his lifetime; his
example of virtue and order as revitalizing now as in his own day.
Hence we may cull from his life and doctrine a number of emphases
that remain perennially relevant.

First, we must mention Maistre's religious position, for in it we
find most of the principles and corollaries that taken together com-
prise the basis of his thought. By religious position, we do not refer
to his Catholic orthodoxy alone but to the amalgam of elements
from which his religious understanding was formed. As we know, he
gathered honey from many flowers. But despite the varied sources—
not to mention the varied genres, the occasional nature of much of
his *oeuvre*, and all the nuance, irony, and paradox he employed—his
thought remained consistent both in outline and detail.

On the one hand, Maistre stood firm in his Catholicism, firm in
basic principles that did not change, though he avoided the pitfall
of hidebound intransigence. He was too subtle of a writer and
thinker to succumb to the temptation of mere reaction. His doctrine was the result of a creative synthesis, wherein one finds both
the influence of past luminaries and hints of developments to come.
Plato, Pascal, Descartes, Bossuet, Leibniz, Cudworth, Francis de
Sales, and Fénelon—these are a few of the earlier notables who
make their appearance even as one detects, according to historian

Owen Bradley, anticipations of nineteenth century figures such as Lamennais, Baudelaire, and Renan.

In addition to orthodox verities, of course, Maistre enhanced his doctrine by employing esoteric currents of thought, a subsidiary stream of surprisingly rich materials not commonly found in the pages of a man of orthodox principle. These materials ranged from Alexandrian theology and Neo-Platonism to alchemy and Freemasonry. By investigating and then using these sources he unified the exoteric and esoteric heritages of the Western world in a manner both original and fruitful.

Maistre's religious traditionalism, then, differed significantly from that of other conservative thinkers in its "markedly intellectual Neoplatonic and Masonic accent."[1] Though welcoming the ideas of non-mainstream figures, he paid only limited attention to the anti-pagan purifiers of the early church, favoring instead such figures as Clement, Origen, Dionysius the Areopagite, and the pagan Greek elements retained in their theologies. We do not find in his spirituality any lessening of Christian faith or principle but rather an imaginative synthesizing (not *syncretizing*) of compatible ingredients, such that Christian dogmas are not weakened or diminished but rather enriched by their addition. Moreover, such Hellenistic borrowings were augmented by universalist elements, a reflection of Maistre's Masonic principles. All in all, his conservative but imaginative Catholicism lacked the intolerance that characterized much of the Restoration community.

We have also recounted how Maistre's life and doctrine bear surprising parallels to those of René Guénon, the twentieth century master of traditional religious and metaphysical principles. Both of these men discerned a metaphysical unity beneath the varied expressions of the world religions; both were enthusiasts of Freemasonry and its social and religious possibilities; both explored the domain of sacred science and its continuing significance; both investigated esoteric teachings and engaged in esoteric disciplines; both were alienated from the popular shibboleths of their day; both refused to subordinate religious truth to the latest claims of natural

1. Owen Bradley, *A Modern Maistre*, 189.

science, and both left their native lands for a life of exile, albeit under very different circumstances.

As a comparatively recent figure, Guénon remains a continuing influence on traditional and conservative modes of thought. A principal goal of this book has been to show that Maistre, though a more distant figure, has much to contribute, also. Yet this claim of relevance is not accepted by all observers. The German historian Klaus Epstein, for example, believed otherwise in the case of Maistre and of conservative thinkers generally. It was his contention that conservatism usually appears as the defense of a specific, concrete, and ever-changing status quo, and is therefore as varied as the conditions it defends. "Its thinkers—excepting the special case of Burke—rarely exercise much influence outside their own countries and times," he wrote, "whether one thinks of Coleridge in England, Maistre and Bonald in France, or Möser, Müller, and Haller in Germany."[2]

No doubt this is a sound generalization but in the case of Maistre, we beg to differ. Partial to our subject as we are, we fully believe his legacy is neither time-bound nor place-bound; rather, it is relevant— where it is known—in more than one era and more than one nation or culture. We believe, for example, that both his political and social observations remain pertinent, not as a blueprint for crafting a nation or society—God forbid—but for their astuteness in understanding human behavior and cultural dynamics. And, as already indicated, we believe his religious, esotericist, and metaphysical thought has a unique and ongoing value, thus separating him from the exclusively political theorists among conservative thinkers past and present. It is his doctrine of religion especially—of spiritually permanent or perennial things—that renders him of special utility in countering the secularizing influences at work in the Western world.[3]

2. Epstein, *The Genesis of German Conservatism* (Princeton, NJ: Princeton University Press, 1966), 7.

3. In our research, we have encountered other counter-revolutionary figures who bear interesting parallels to Maistre, including the Dutchmen Abraham Kuyper (who was much influenced by the theosophist Franz von Baader) and Groen van Prinsterer (who penned a lengthy treatise attacking the French Revolution), and the Prussian reformer, Johann Christoph Wöllner. See appendix two for more on these Christian statesmen.

In turning to Maistre's convictions regarding Providence, we come to a subject of surpassing importance yet one handled with the usual light touch. One of the many serious claims he made on behalf of the workings of Providence, albeit made in a most unserious manner, appears in a letter to Mme. De Costa written in 1793, several months before the French Revolution descended into the "Reign of Terror." "Human idiocy and perfidy," he writes, "are two immense blind men of which Madame Providence makes use to arrive at her goals, as an artist makes use of a tool to execute his works." Providence, therefore, does not shun the most foolish and vicious of agents as "tools" in her projects to craft historical dramas and outcomes. Not that Providence uses only substandard agents of the race; she also uses the wise and virtuous, depending on the purpose to be attained. In the case of France, she wielded her scourge upon the lives of a people who had sown the wind of revolution and reaped the whirlwind. "Does the file know that it is making a key?" Maistre asks. "All the execrable and laughable personages who act in this moment on the world's stage are files. When the work is done, we will prostrate ourselves to receive it from the hands of the Great Worker."[4] Thus France receives judgment at the hand of God the "Great Worker," a phrase evoking an alchemical motif, as Providence spiritually transmutes material events—the events of the Revolution in all their pathos—for the ultimate benefit of humanity, hard as it might be to see any benefit amidst the violence and folly of the unfolding drama.

In treating of religion more generally, Maistre, as we have seen, applied his insights extensively to political developments and related social behavior, as in his writings on the Revolution. In doing so, he assigned an important and pragmatic role to the mythologies of peoples, to "myths" as commonly held legendary stories conveying the words and deeds of heroes and deities. Without myth (or religion), so to speak, the people perish. He insisted that history proves "that religion is necessary to the peoples, and that [for example] the Sermon on the Mount will always be regarded as an acceptable code of morals." Though favoring something of a pragmatic approach, he

4. Bradley, *A Modern Maistre*, 192.

cautioned that mythologies must be consistent to have influence. "If its dogmas are fables, it is necessary at least that there be *unity of fables*, which will never happen without *unity of doctrine* and authority, which in turn becomes impossible without the supremacy of the sovereign pontiff." Here he takes a swipe at the non-Catholic world, wherein unity of doctrine and authority had become nearly impossible. He adds rather cynically that if he were an atheist and a sovereign, he would nonetheless "declare the pope infallible, by public edict, for the establishment and security of peace in my estates."[5]

In addition to the need for religious agreement, Maistre echoes Plato in saying that civil order also depends on a belief in justice as both a this-worldly and an otherworldly phenomenon, and that even if it were only the latter, there would be no "more useful fiction than this . . . for the sake of its effect on the young." In respect of faith in one's national dogmas and in Providence, Maistre again cites Plato, who declared that "one must believe these things on faith from the legislators and the antique traditions, at least if one has lost the spirit."[6] One could never accuse Maistre of disdaining *realpolitik* but one must not be led to believe his own religious faith was anything but genuine.

So too were his convictions regarding Freemasonry, though he did abrogate some of his enthusiasm in the *Soirées*. His congenial experience of the lodges as a young man, however, remained with him throughout his life, even during later years when it was difficult if not impossible to participate actively in Masonry. His active participation had begun in 1772 and lasted to 1793, or from the age of nineteen to the age of forty. His somewhat dismissive remarks about Masonry as a social opportunity for like-minded individuals cannot be taken as anything but a light-hearted observation of an incontestable reality, for indeed lodge affiliation allowed camaraderie to all members while only some members sought the deeper character and perspectives of the organization. His 1778 initiation into La Sincérité, a highly esoteric lodge in which he rose to the highest grades, not only proves the seriousness of his attachment but also demon-

5. Ibid., 195. Letter to the archevêque de Severoli, December, 1, 1815.
6. Ibid. Quotations from *The Laws II*.

strates his interest in Orientalist cosmology and arcane ritual, as well as indicating a pre-Romantic sensibility that would temper earlier influences from his copious Enlightenment reading.

In writing of Freemasonry, Maistre provided later generations with a balanced but favorable awareness of Masonry and its strengths, while correcting some of its apparent deficits in the eyes of Catholic and other Christian believers. It is important to note that his belief and practice as a Mason, along with his hope for the Masonic "mission," was a religious one, tied irrevocably to Christian belief. Moreover, it enriched that belief with a spiritual interiority that too often seemed lacking in the latter half of the eighteenth century.

In addition, Maistre made the case that Masonry was not the cause of the French Revolution, despite conspiracy theories assigning blame to secret societies of Masons and German Illuminati. Such theories were at the least exaggerated, and the many lodges given only to ritual and symbolism, philanthropy and hope for social progress were quite innocent of any such designs. Maistre's attempt to distinguish good and bad Masonry—to him the good could only be Christian while the bad allied itself with rationalism and the Revolution—remains useful to today's readers but has been unable to remove the taint applied by Catholic writers of the early nineteenth century, who rendered Masonry suspect in the eyes of the faithful. Still, Maistre's self-appointed role as an architect of Christian renewal, and his enlistment of Masonry in that cause, is instructive to all who wish to be fair in discerning Masonry's contributions and possibilities.

As observed in chapter three, René Guénon was equally as ardent about promoting Masonry in the twentieth century as Maistre had been in the eighteenth. However, unlike Maistre, Guénon's experiences in Masonic lodges were clearly of a mixed nature, as some of the organizations he belonged to in his early years were of dubious paternity. Even so, he remained convinced of the legitimacy of Masonry's traditional doctrine and practice and its potentials for the future. In fact, for a time he looked to two institutions, Masonry and the Catholic Church, as principal sources of renewal for a decadent West, although he later resigned himself to the fact that neither—in their current form—were capable of successfully undertaking such a task.

Though at first glance, Masonry and Catholicism might appear as the oddest of bedfellows, Guénon perceived things from an esoteric point of view—as things both "seen and unseen"—and thus discerned complementary virtues and resources in both of them. (Maistre had done much the same thing well over a century earlier.) In Guénon's view, Christianity was one of the divinely revealed and thereby authentic religions, and for centuries the Catholic Church had been its institutional representative in the West. Thus for Guénon, Catholicism was an easy choice as a vehicle of renewal. Guénon saw Masonry as an equally valid—though distinct—form of renewal, having been useful in the past for its ability to initiate its members; that is, to inaugurate and facilitate their spiritual realization. Both Catholicism and Masonry, then, owing to their initiatic potentials, as well as to their universalism and transcendentalism, were not unlikely recommendations. Though different on the exoteric level, esoteric themes intertwined beneath the surface.

Masonry thus provided Maistre and Guénon with symbolic links to a primordial tradition, a tradition out of which had descended a variety of enduring religions both East and West. From such ancient streams of spiritual tradition they fashioned their systems. Maistre enhanced his Masonic esotericism with the now familiar complements of Neoplatonism and Origenist theology, not to mention the Hebrew and Christian revelations. For his part, Guénon looked further afield to round out his Masonic theory, integrating it as he did with the metaphysical schema he had crafted from the Hindu philosophy of Vedanta. Hence Masons to this day who look to the East look also to Guénon, for in many instances he interpreted Masonic symbols in light of traditional Eastern teachings. Though he did not deny the reality of a Western esoteric tradition, he believed it to be "almost completely obscured by the growth of anti-traditional ways of thought, while eastern tradition has been better preserved."[7]

Although an authentic vehicle of tradition in earlier times, then,

---

7. Jean Borella, "René Guénon and the Traditionalist School," *Modern Esoteric Spirituality*, 273.

the prevailing intellectual confusion in the West had rendered Masonry's esoteric teaching and its initiatory capability, in Guénon's view, largely ineffectual. This being said, both Maistre and Guénon conveyed in their writings much useful knowledge of Masonry and its potentials, and thus introduced their readers to the same. For that reason, persons today who might otherwise dismiss Masonry as merely an out-of-date, innocuous fraternal organization, complete with odd rituals, funny regalia, and secret handshakes, are able to assess more knowledgeably its doctrines and rituals, at least where (and if) these are taught and practiced in a more-or-less traditional manner.

Returning more specifically to Maistre himself, we must take note of the Count's polemical abilities in regard to belief and unbelief in religion. His attachment to this task runs through much of his work and serves to equip his readers with spiritual and psychological insights that remain useful today. The *Soirées* is a gold mine of such insights, as its three-way dialogue provides for the airing of various perspectives on religious, social, and philosophical themes. At the very beginning of the first dialogue, the Count (Maistre's mouthpiece) says he wishes he had been able to say with Montaigne that man "fools himself," a comment that is "exactly right." For it is quite true, Maistre says (in regard to skepticism), that man "is his own dupe; he takes the sophisms of his naturally rebellious heart (alas, nothing is more certain) for real doubts born of his understanding. If occasionally superstition *believes in belief*, as it is accused of, more often still, you can be sure, *pride believes in disbelief*. In both cases, man *fools himself*, but in the second this is much worse."[8] Here Maistre pricks the vanity of the unbeliever, who rationalizes his unbelief by claiming it derives from a rigorous investigation of the relevant questions, when in fact it does no such thing. Rather, his unbelief conforms to presuppositions already fixed in his mind, and of which he is probably unaware, thinking instead that his Olympian grasp of objective reality is the unbiased source of his convictions.

8. *The Saint Petersburg Dialogues*, in *The Works of Joseph de Maistre*, trans. Jack Lively, 183.

Later in the dialogue, the Count takes aim once again at non-believers, referencing "the unfortunate [David] Hume" and "the Spinoza of Voltaire," who said to God, "*Just between ourselves I believe that you do not exist.*" The skeptic claims, declares the Count, that the existence of evil is an argument against the existence of God, for if he existed, evil and its injustice would not themselves exist. One way or another, then, such men think they know *the God who does not exist* is somehow *just by nature*; that is, they somehow know the attributes of a chimerical being, and are ready to tell everyone in detail just how God would behave if, by chance, there *was* a God. "In truth," the Count says, "there could be no more well-seasoned folly. If one could laugh on such a sad subject, who could refrain on hearing men, who have surely a head on their shoulders like us, argue against God using the very idea he has given to them of himself, without their thinking that this idea alone proves the existence of God, since one cannot have an idea of something that does not exist?" Thus to deny God the atheist assumes him, since man conceives only what exists.[9] The foregoing reminds us of a similar argument made by the twentieth-century Christian apologist, C. S. Lewis.[10]

In exposing the logical deficiencies—if not the intentional dissembling—of skeptics and scoffers, Maistre was both subtle and

9. Ibid., 263.

10. *Mere Christianity* (New York: Macmillan Publishing Co., Inc., 1976), 45–46. Even if they deny it, Lewis asserted, men somehow know that cruelty, injustice, and meaninglessness are but part of the picture. "My argument against God," he wrote, "was that the universe seemed so cruel and unjust. But how had I got this idea of *just* and *unjust*? A man does not call a line crooked unless he has some idea of a straight line. What was I comparing this universe with when I called it unjust? If the whole show was bad and senseless from A to Z... why did I, who was supposed to be part of the show, find myself in such violent reaction against it?" He continued by saying he could have given up his idea of justice by allowing it was nothing more than a private idea of his own. "But if I did that," he said, "then my argument against God collapsed too—for the argument depended on saying that the world was really unjust, not simply that it did not happen to please my private fancies. Thus in the very act of trying to prove that God did not exist—in other words, that the whole of reality was senseless—I found I was forced to assume that one part of reality—namely my idea of justice—was full of sense." Thus, he concluded, if the whole universe has no meaning, one would never have found out that it has no meaning.

adroit. He was equally skilled in criticizing superficial theists whom he found defective in their understanding. Two more examples should suffice. (Again, the Count of the *Soirées* presents the argument.) Allowing that God is the "legislator" of the universe, he therefore asks what might be an injustice of God in regard to men? (For non-believers often accused *the God in whom they did not believe* of being unjust in his treatment of the human race, even as certain theists were absurdly ignorant of the truth regarding the God in whom they *did believe*.) "Is there by any chance," the Count asks, "some common legislator above God who prescribes to him the way in which he should act toward men? And who will be the judge between this being and ourselves?"[11]

Further on, the Count asks to be allowed "to set up this impressive argument," which posits a deity who is unjust, cruel, pitiless; a deity who enjoys the unhappiness of his creatures; therefore—"here I pay attention to the grumblers," he says—there is apparently no reason to pray to him. But on the contrary, he replies, there is nothing more obvious and necessary than "*to pray to him and serve him with much more zeal and care* than if his mercy was without bounds, as we think is the case." Here follows an analogy to illustrate the argument. "If you had lived under the rule of a prince," the Count supposes, "not, you will note, wicked, but only severe, touchy, never easy in his authority, and seeking to supervise every movement of his subjects, I am curious to know if you would have thought yourself able to take the same liberties as under the rule of another prince of a wholly opposite character, content with general liberty, always tender of individual freedom, and always fearing his own power so that no one else should fear it?" The answer is simple enough. "The more terrible God seems to us [though in fact Maistre found God's ways just and merciful though often enough inscrutable], the more we must increase our religious fear of him, the more ardent and indefatigable must be our prayers, for there is no reason for us to think that his goodness will make up for our ignoring them." Such are among the arguments that Maistre used to

---

11. *The Saint Petersburg Dialogues,* trans. Jack Lively, 267.

refute "the complaints that the foolhardy have raised against Providence."[12]

Speaking of prayer, Maistre was never lacking in either conviction or speculation. "I understand perfectly," the Count declares, "not only that prayer is useful in general in warding off physical evil, but that it is the true antidote, the natural specific, for it and that in its essence it tends to destroy it." This bold pronouncement is followed by another, in which he looks at prayer from the point of view of its effects as a secondary cause, indistinguishable from other secondary causes. If a "fashionable philosopher," convinced solely of material necessity, should be surprised to hear the Count use prayer to protect himself against lightning, the Count would reply as follows: *"And why do you, sir, use lightning rods? Or, to restrict myself to something more usual, Why do you use fire engines in fires and medicines in illnesses? Are you not setting your face against eternal laws quite as much as I am?"* The philosopher would then protest that the Count's examples are quite a different thing, "for if it is a law . . . that fire burns, it is also a law that water puts out fire." Not to be outdone, the Count replies in kind, for that *"is exactly what I say for my part, for if it is a law that lightning produces a certain catastrophe, it is also a law that prayer, sprinkled in time on the* HEAVENLY FIRE, *extinguishes or diverts it."* Satisfied with this riposte, he concludes by assuring his antagonists "there is no objection of this kind that I cannot counter to my advantage: there is no mid-point between a rigid, absolute, and universal fatalism and the wide-spread faith of men in the efficacy of prayer."[13]

Turning to a more worldly subject, though not for that reason a subject beyond the guiding hand of Providence, we must consider Maistre's political acumen. Unlike the Royalists of France who sought to exact vengeance against the Revolutionaries who had dispossessed them, Maistre advised a milder and more realistic type of restoration. Keenly aware of the ineptitude of the Bourbons, and equally aware that France could never restore an epoch that had forever passed from the scene, he found himself at odds with his fellow

12. Ibid., 267–68.
13. Ibid., 226–27.

Royalists in mapping a strategy for counterrevolution. Indeed, he advised against a counterrevolution—that is, a revolution in reverse —while recommending "passage from violence to order, from sickness to health, vice to virtue."[14] The strategy arose from his theory of compensations, which held that restoration should result in a return to equilibrium and avoidance of retribution. The process would be something like convalescence from a destructive and deserved illness. For Maistre was always adamant in viewing the Revolution as a punishment for the sins of the people, as "the work of every vice" as it recoiled on its perpetrators and the millions who supported them either actively or passively.[15]

Maistre's strategy was based on principles similar to those advanced a century later by René Guénon in the latter's discussion of war and justice. These same principles remain as valid today as they were at the beginning of the nineteenth century and the first half of the twentieth century, as Europe and America continue to wrestle with latter-day Enlightenment philosophical extensions and their progressive and left-leaning purveyors. The keys to Maistre's and Guénon's views on the subject are found in compensation—as noted above—and equilibrium. As in physics every action has an equal and opposite reaction, so too in human events. For when the agents of disorder challenge or overthrow the agents of order, the former provoke a reaction—often in the form of organized violence—from the agents of order. In Guénon's view, then, war is directed against those who create disorder, with the intention of returning them to order. This is a legitimate function, he says, "which is in fact nothing other than an aspect of the function of justice, understood in its most general sense."[16] Indeed, it was sustained warfare over a period of twenty years, waged by royal powers against the armies of the Revolution and its Napoleonic prolongation, which finally restored to the heart of Europe an equilibrium ruptured initially by the maelstrom in France.

14. Bradley, *A Modern Maistre*, 220.
15. Ibid.
16. *Fundamental Symbols: The Universal Language of Sacred Science* (Cambridge, UK: Quinta Essentia, 1995), 129.

Realizing that the French Revolution had inaugurated changes that could or would never be revoked, Maistre viewed the return to equilibrium as ushering in a largely new state of affairs rather than a restoration of the previous era. History never stands still and never repeats itself in full measure. Even successful counterrevolutions absorb and assimilate many of the changes wrought by interregnum powers. Hence Maistre's recommendations against counterrevolutionary violence (at least beyond the necessary violence already alluded to), which could only perpetuate the violence of the Revolution and condemn the legitimate party to the role of permanent counterpart in a never-ending back-and-forth struggle with the illegitimate party. Better a strategy in which the Revolution's poisoned fruit could be transmuted into something healthy, in which the king (in this case, an heir of the deposed Louis XVI) could be recognized and accepted by the people. In this as in so much else, Maistre was a realist. Acutely aware by 1814–15 that the Revolution itself had become a tradition, he was cautious and clear-eyed in regard to the extent that any restoration would be able to reverse all or many of its changes. More than a dozen years earlier, he had realized that a full return to the *Ancien Régime* would be "much more mad than putting Lake Geneva in bottles."[17]

So much for politics; for the rising and falling of states and peoples. Through it all, Maistre retained a composure and objectivity that did him credit. His personal attributes were rooted in the permanent things, thus foreign invasion, revolutionary excess, exile from his homeland, loss of status, loss of property, and the passing of an epoch—though acutely painful to him—were transcended by the theological virtues that underpinned his character. Unfailingly, he was a man guided not only by a keen mind but a good heart, knowing the truth both rationally and intuitively, and living according to it.

It was one of his favorite ideas, he wrote, "that the upright man is very commonly informed, by an inner sentiment, of the falsity or truth of certain propositions before any examination, often even

17. Bradley, *A Modern Maistre*, 224. Letter to Vignet des Etoles, 9 December 1793.

without having made the studies necessary to be in a position to examine them with full knowledge of the case."[18] Maistre was of this stamp. This did not mean, however, that he self-righteously placed himself above and beyond the common clay of humanity. He knew that even the upright man is a sinner, torn from within. "I do not know what the heart of a rascal may be"; he famously said, "I know what is in the heart of an honest man; it is horrible." Yet the honest man faces that which others hardly dare entertain in the deepest recesses of their minds. In Maistre, an undiluted honesty flowed through the veins, intrinsic to the man. Instinctively aware of the falsity or truth of certain propositions, sensitive to the cant and evasions of others, he spoke with veracity and wit of all that claimed his attention.

He spoke, he acted, he waited. Long years he waited, dispossessed, exiled, yet not without hope. With others of a "truly religious" bent, he awaited "a huge event in the divine order," an extraordinary event, a sign from heaven. Perhaps, he speculated prophetically, a man of genius would appear, a man whose mind possessed natural affinities for both religion and science. Yet whatever it might be, Maistre insisted, all indications favored a prodigy of some sort, an agent of restoration and renewal to sweep away the century of the *philosophes*, to mock that century's stupidities even as contemporaries mocked the superstitions of the Middle Ages. Those who waited prepared for the event by engaging in "holy studies," by "excavating . . . seams of grace and divine goodness." At the time of fruition, Maistre declared, "The spirit, for long dethroned and forgotten, will take its former position. It will be shown that all the ancient traditions are true, that the whole of paganism is nothing but a system of tainted and ill-conceived truths which need only cleaning, so to speak, and restoring to their place to shine brilliantly. In a word, all ideas will be changed."[19]

On that prophetic if enigmatic note, appearing near the end of the posthumously published *Soirées*, Maistre offered a vision in which religion—the transcendent link binding heaven and earth—

18. *The Saint Petersburg Dialogues,* trans. Jack Lively, 185.
19. Ibid., 288, 289.

would again hold sway in the affairs of men. He believed the time was near. Men, he held, could not live indefinitely in a state of irreligion. Pessimist though he was, he could not abandon all hope. Late as the hour may have been, the portents bade well for the future.

Appendix I
Maistre and Isaiah Berlin

ISAIAH BERLIN'S ESSAY[1] on Joseph de Maistre, written in 1960 and lightly revised for publication thirty years later, links the name of the Savoyard author and philosopher with the word "fascism," a word guaranteed to cast a malevolent shadow over Maistre and all his works. Yet aside from the title of the essay, Berlin's treatment of Maistre is largely measured and fair-minded. This is not to let the eminent philosopher of ideas off the hook but to give him his due. Clearly his own liberal bias is at work in the essay, but erudition and balance are on display also.

Early in his eighty-three page essay, Berlin cites a number of critics who present a stock portrait of the Count, based largely on the inventions of Sainte-Beuve in the nineteenth century. To his credit, he dismisses these distortions and exaggerations before painting his own portrait of Maistre. He also dismisses those who liken Maistre to the counter-revolutionary Louis Bonald, observing that Maistre's ideas were bolder and more original than those of the reactionary Bonald, whose predictable support of ultramontane theocracy was narrow in scope though admittedly rigorous and clear in principle. By contrast, Berlin asserts that Maistre was no advocate of reaction but instead a seer, a visionary, a prophet. Having pilloried the views of much Enlightenment philosophy and the revolutionary excesses that followed in their wake, he foresaw the chaos and violence that would mark their heritage in future generations. Nor did he share the backward-looking perspective of contemporary English tradi-

---

1. "Joseph de Maistre and the Origins of Fascism" in *The Crooked Timber of Humanity: Chapters in the History of Ideas*, ed. Henry Hardy (Princeton NJ: Princeton University Press, 1990). By linking not only Maistre's name but the word "origin" with fascism, the title is doubly suggestive and problematic.

tionalists and German Romantics, whose understanding of human- ity—quixotically conservative in some aspects—was more or less benign and largely free of pessimism. Theirs was the opposite of Maistre's position, informed as it was by the sense of original sin, which saw humanity left to itself—in Berlin's exaggerated terms— as characterized by "wickedness and worthlessness" and "self- destructive stupidity."[2]

If at odds with both counter-revolutionaries and Romantics, then, we suggest Maistre would have been equally at odds with fas- cism, were it in existence in his day. For this militant ideology, born of the inhumanities of World War One, never preached original sin or human limitation but rather the glorious destiny of superior peoples, a bright future of unity and purity once inner and outer enemies had been crushed and the people purged of decadent influ- ences. Descriptors of the fascist project, never quite the same in any two countries, include radical nationalism, revolutionary spirit, authoritarianism or totalitarianism, heroic idealism, militarism, populism, vitalism, political violence, mass mobilization, a regu- lated economy, anti-liberalism *and* anti-conservatism, plus vari- ables such as anti-Semitism and other forms of racism. Anti- communism is another identifier, though anachronistic in Maistre's case. Of the foregoing, one could charge Maistre with anti-liberal- ism and perhaps cast him as an authoritarian (but not one who favored unchecked power). With the rest, he would have nothing to do. Even the measured violence of the state so vividly described in his works indicates no desire to apply it beyond the necessities posed by criminal behavior or foreign invasion. He never glorified state violence; his kind and generous nature abhorred its abuse.

Additionally, Maistre dismissed as overdrawn the heroism and will to power of the "great man," the man who overcomes the odds, rises to the top, and leads his people to triumph over enemies within and without. As Berlin observes, Maistre believed that men who seize power do not really know how they have done so. Such men do not realize that circumstances, which they neither foresee nor direct, do everything for them without their assistance. For

2. Ibid., 115.

behind the scenes, Providence decrees its unsearchable judgments and pursues its inscrutable ends.

More than three-fourths of the way through the essay, Berlin takes a harsher tone in his critique. There he takes up—and finds merit in—the counterintuitive notion of the Saint-Simonian School, put forward five years after the Count's death, that Maistre and Voltaire were cut from the same cloth, despite their wide and irreconcilable philosophical differences. "Modern totalitarian systems do," Berlin suggests, "in their acts if not in their style of rhetoric, combine the outlooks of Voltaire and Maistre.... For, polar opposites as they are, they both belong to the tough-minded tradition in classical French thought."[3] In spite of the opposition of their ideas, then, "the quality of mind is often exceedingly similar.... Neither Voltaire nor his enemy is guilty of any degree of softness, vagueness or self-indulgence of either intellect or feeling, nor do they tolerate it in others." Instead, they stand for "the dry light against the flickering flame"; they oppose all that is turbid, misty, and impressionistic. Not for them the eloquence of Rousseau, Chateaubriand, Hugo, Michelet, Bergson, Péguy. They are "ruthlessly deflationary writers, contemptuous, sardonic, genuinely heartless and, at times, genuinely cynical."[4]

By the cast of their minds, Berlin says, one can trace their true descendants in figures such as Marx, Tolstoy, Sorel, and Lenin. Although Berlin presents but a tiny sample, it is surprising that he mentions not a single fascist in this diverse foursome. Only Georges Sorel could be accused of proto-fascist ideas, particularly on the regenerative nature of violence and his very brief association with Charles Maurras's *Action française*, but in fact he was a syndicalist, had publicly declared his position as a Marxist and a socialist, and was an admirer of Lenin.

Thus it seems to be less the peculiar character of fascism, read backwards into the Count's own time and place, than twentieth century totalitarianism more broadly that stands accused of assimilating Maistrian influences. Although Berlin blames Maistre for

3. Ibid., 159.
4. Ibid.

holding that government is unworkable without "perpetual repression of the weak and confused majority by a minority of dedicated rulers," he fails to link this notion—formulated in his words, not Maistre's—to either fascism or Marxism or Maistre. He does claim that Maistre's ideas "approach the strong strain of nihilism in all modern totalitarianism," but this too appears highly debatable. For despite his historicism, political pragmatism, and low estimate of human capacity and goodness (Berlin's formulations again), Maistre never confused his point of view with suggestions of nihilism, that is, with total rejectionism, meaninglessness, dismissal of an objective basis for truth, or any other general definition of the term. Maistre found the world anything but meaningless, suffused as it was by awareness of God's providence.

Berlin continues by observing that such thinkers as Kant, Mill, and Russell—unlike Maistre—seek to convince others by rational arguments. These philosophers insist that if their arguments are exposed by counter-arguments as fallacious, they are willing to regard themselves as mistaken. Berlin suggests thinkers of a more metaphysical type, however, among them Plato, Berkeley, Hegel, and Marx, use rational arguments as mere auxiliaries to their purpose, that purpose being to expound all-embracing conceptions of the world and man's place in it in order to transform the vision of those who hear their ideas, not to convince them of their impeccable logic. They strive "not so much to convince as to convert," to bring those whom they address to a new perspective, to make them see the facts in a new light or from a new angle, "in terms of a new pattern in which what had earlier seemed to be a casual amalgam of elements is presented as a systematic, interrelated unity."[5]

Berlin follows these assertions by describing Maistre as a dogmatic thinker "whose ultimate principles and premises nothing can shake, and whose considerable ingenuity and intellectual power are devoted to making the facts fit his preconceived notions, not to developing concepts which fit newly discovered, or newly visualized, facts."[6] Maistre is like a lawyer arguing a brief, he says; the con-

5. Ibid., 161–62.
6. Ibid., 162.

clusion is foregone and he knows he must arrive at it somehow, for he is convinced of its truth. Of course, Maistre had been a magistrate and the habits of the law court were formed early in life. Yet his philosophical "brief" was no more or less set in stone than anyone else's. We do not claim he did not reason from first principles but rather contend that *everyone* reasons from first principles, consciously or unconsciously. He merely held a different set of first principles—or presuppositions—than did Berlin. For Berlin reasoned and argued as a liberal, an eloquent and learned liberal but a liberal nonetheless. Ever so subtly he committed an error that many modern secular or humanistic thinkers commit, which is to fail to recognize their own presuppositions while identifying those of others. For the liberal has his own foundational beliefs, his own axioms, which prefigure and determine all others.[7]

Although Maistre was prone to occasional exaggeration to startle or convince his readers, and although he was hardly infallible in his judgments and ideas, Berlin's insistence on his "irrationalism"—his religious belief or his assertion of innate ideas, for example— appears to us to be an exaggeration itself. Like others of the same point of view, Berlin was incapable of experiencing religious faith in any of its traditional expressions. Absent such a capacity and the perspective it provides, we suggest he was unable to "get inside" religious faith or to see it as occupying anything but an "irrational" position. Despite Berlin's stated respect for his own tradition of Judaism, it seems he viewed religion as generally based on preju-

7. One of Berlin's foundational beliefs was unbelief, so to speak, which is no small matter when dealing with a subject—Maistre in this case—for whom religious belief was of central importance. Not that Berlin was unable to appreciate religious believers or understand—after a fashion—their reasons for belief, or that he was consciously unfair to those who did believe, but clearly his position lent a bias to his writings. In the mid-1960s, during an informal conversation at Oxford with a visiting scholar from America, Berlin acknowledged he "wanted to, but could not, bring himself to believe" in his ancestral Judaism. According to the same source (James Cracraft, professor emeritus of history at the University of Illinois at Chicago), Berlin also confided his great respect for Jewish religious tradition, with which he was intimately acquainted. As a child in Riga, he had attended Hebrew school and, as an adult, he was a fluent reader of classical Hebrew texts. He was also an ardent Zionist. (Personal recollection as told to the author, January 2016.)

dice, wishful thinking, or outmoded metaphysical ideas, whatever practical benefits it might provide.[8]

These considerations may appear to take us far afield but we believe they cast light on differences in sensibility and principle separating the agnostic liberal—no matter how learned and wise in terms of secular perspective—and the religious believer, who anchors himself in a domain transcending reason, yet who also finds reason an indispensable tool both theoretically and practically. That Berlin reasons from the presuppositions of the first position—whether acknowledged or not—we think determines much of what he thinks of Maistre's point of view. His horizons were thus limited because reason by itself is a receptive faculty not a creative power. His world was a smaller one than Maistre's, a world incapable of surpassing its self-limiting perspectives or fully appreciating those who can.

Moreover, Berlin's tone and content in the Maistre essay, largely measured and fair-minded as we have already observed, may not have adequately reflected his overall view of Maistre. In the interests of balanced scholarship, he may have resisted the temptation to present too one-sided a view of his subject, who would after all have appeared to Berlin as someone almost completely at odds with his own political and religious views and overall sense of life. At other times and places, he was harsher in his comments. As illustration, we have culled several quotations from his introduction to Richard

---

8. Ironically, such secular thinking is not unrelated to the scholastic exercises of the Middle Ages, which centered on logic alone and not on the intuitive grasp of truth. They were essentially a defense against error, not a means to realizing and appropriating truths from a higher domain. (Those truths were largely established already by religious dogma.) So, too, much of Greek thought took aim at providing causal explanations pursued disinterestedly on the level of speculative logic, rather than seeking to understand the means to full realization of personal being. Modernist thought, increasingly detached from roots in the transcendental domain, has left profane reason stranded in relativity, to which in turn it has reduced every element of absoluteness. Certainty is beyond its grasp; all things beyond the empirical use of reason informed by experience are reduced to the subjective and relative domain, not counting an illogical exception in favor of this reduction itself. Yet if a man is able to doubt, it suggests there is certainty; if he is able to experience illusion, it suggests there is access to reality.

Lebrun's 1994 translation of *Considerations on France*.[9] Maistre defended in that work, Berlin asserts, "the importance of mystery, of darkness, almost of ignorance, and above all of irrationality, as the basis of social and political life. With immense effectiveness and brilliance he denounced every form of lucidity, every form of rationality." Elsewhere, he says, he was temperamentally "as ruthless and as extreme as his great enemies, the Jacobins." In addition, he says Maistre "attacked eighteenth-century rationalism with the intolerance and the passion and the power and the gusto of the great revolutionaries themselves. He wanted to destroy what has been so well called 'the heavenly city of the eighteenth century philosophers.'" In these quotations one indeed recognizes aspects of Maistre and his message but presented in such a way that, lacking proper context, they convey half-truths and exaggerated implications, thus painting a one-sided picture. Now Berlin may have thought he was painting a balanced portrait of the man, and convinced liberal that he was, he probably thought just this, but in fact we do not believe this to be the case.

When all has been said, neither Maistre's basic principles nor occasional lurid descriptions of human or natural violence should have linked his name and legacy to fascism. Berlin himself—in the essay not the title of the essay—does little to connect Maistre with fascism as such; rather, as we have seen, he links him more generally—and tenuously—to various totalitarian systems of a later period, be they communist or fascist or national socialist. Yet even these connections appear to us to be mistaken. For Maistre's Catholicism, enriched by perennial influences and esoteric insights, did not in fact lend itself to sanctioning the lawless ideological systems that so plagued the twentieth century.

9. Lebrun, *Considerations*, xvi.

Appendix II
Tradition in
the Protestant World

EDMUND BURKE'S seminal conservatism was clearly the British counterpart to Joseph de Maistre's continental conservatism. One could say he was also the Protestant counterpart to the Roman Catholic Maistre, though his specifically religious views reflected a less spiritual sensibility than Maistre's, whose piety appears to have been deeper and more heartfelt. Protestant parallels closer than the Anglican Burke can be found in the Lutheran Johann Christoph von Wöllner and the Calvinist Abraham Kuyper, each of whom we shall consider here. They resemble Maistre (and Réne Guénon) in major ways, specifically their religious orthodoxy (in the sense of core Christian doctrine), conservative political views, and esotericist inclinations. One could no doubt find additional figures of equal significance to our principal subjects but these two possess too many similarities to go unmentioned.

Wöllner (1732–1800), only a generation older than Maistre, encountered many of the same Enlightenment currents as did the younger man. An orthodox Lutheran, a Freemason, and a Rosicrucian, he was a trusted and influential advisor during the reign of Frederick William II of Prussia. Contrarily, he was despised by the king's predecessor, Frederick II ("Frederick the Great"), who called him a "treacherous and intriguing priest." More recently, the everyman's philosopher Will Durant not only repeated Frederick's insult but described Wöllner in broadly unsympathetic terms in a passage friendly to Immanuel Kant. He referred to the "Pietist" Wöllner as one "who divided his time between alchemy and Rosicrucian mysteries, and climbed to power by offering himself as 'an unworthy instrument' to the new monarch's policy of restoring orthodox faith by compulsion." In 1788, he noted, Wöllner "issued a decree which forbade any teaching, in school or university, that deviated from the orthodox form of Lutheran Protestantism; he established a strict censorship over all forms of publication, and ordered the discharge of every teacher suspected of any heresy."[1]

More recently yet, a somewhat more favorable—and hence more balanced—assessment of Wöllner and his project has appeared. Prior to his untimely death in 1967, Klaus Epstein published *The Genesis of German Conservatism*,[2] in which he traced developments from around 1770, when organized political activity of a conservative character appeared in German lands, to 1806, at which time the Holy Roman Empire collapsed. (Despite these early stirrings, it was only after the Napoleonic Wars that conservative parties as such were formed in Germany.)

According to Epstein, then, the Prussian struggle against the German Enlightenment—or *Aufklärung*—began two decades before the start of the French Revolution in 1789, but it was that stupendous event and its lead-up that intensified opposition against progressive currents. During the reign of Frederick the Great, many such currents had been welcomed in Prussia, despite the monarch's absolutist rule. Sympathies changed with Frederick's death in 1786 and the accession to the throne of his sensuous, charming, and rather feckless nephew, Frederick William II. Though unwilling to abolish the absolutist policies of his famous uncle, the new king lacked the strength and ability to perpetuate the Frederician tradition effectively. Nonetheless, capitalizing on a gift for cultivating popularity with his subjects, Frederick William attempted to maintain the status quo with the assistance of a pair of talented ministers.

Enter Johann Christoph Wöllner and Rudolph von Bischoffwerder, the latter a nobleman, cavalryman, and later the stable master and chamberlain to Charles Duke of Courland. He, too, was a Rosicrucian. Not only that, but his Rosicrucian superior was none other than Wöllner himself, a man of humbler origins but with the ambi-

---

1. *The Story of Philosophy* (Garden City, NY: Garden City Publishing Co., Inc., 1933), 305–6.
2. *The Genesis of German Conservatism*, vii.

tion to rise in society. In a career spanning more than three decades, the enterprising Wöllner would indeed achieve personal and public success. In large part, his (and Bischoffwerder's) achievement can be measured by the lengths to which Rosicrucianism became "the semi-official ideology of the once 'enlightened' Prussian state,"[3] alongside his drafting and implementing of royal policy.

So who was this minister of state and dedicated esotericist? Son of a Lutheran pastor, Wöllner initially undertook a clerical career himself but soon abandoned it in favor of a more attractive prospect. This he found as administrator of the landed estates of the socially prominent widow of the late General August Friedrich von Itzenplitz, who had been killed in battle in 1759. In addition to his administrative duties on the estates, Wöllner commenced to write books and reviews on agriculture, becoming an acknowledged authority on the subject. More importantly, he married the General's only daughter in 1766, a match approved by the bride's mother but resented by other members of her Junker family, who clung to the rigid class barriers favored by Frederick II.

In 1770, Wöllner was named rent master and administrator of forests for Prince Henry, a position that allowed him the leisure to indulge his growing interest in secret societies. He had become a Freemason in 1765, subsequently rising to *praepositus* of the five lodges of the Berlin prefecture in 1773 and becoming a Knight of the Strict Observance in 1776. Disappointed "at his failure to learn either deep secrets or to acquire supernatural power,"[4] he left Masonry to become a Rosicrucian in 1779. As with the Masons, he employed social drive and oratorical ability to rise in the organization, soon becoming chief organizer for Northern Germany and *Oberhauptdirektor* in charge of twenty-six *Zirkel* consisting of two-hundred members. Though he attained the eighth Rosicrucian degree, the *magistri*, he complained the "Magi"—whose identity is unknown—refused to initiate him into the final mysteries. According to Epstein, it is unclear in all of this whether Wöllner "was an honest fanatic, an

3. Epstein, *The Genesis of German Conservatism*, 356.
4. Ibid., 357.

unscrupulous opportunist, or a mixture of both."[5] That he was ambitious is beyond a doubt; that he was an unscrupulous opportunist seems unlikely to us. Yet he and his colleague clearly took advantage of the opportunities presented. Even before 1786, the year Frederick William ascended the throne, Wöllner and Bischoffwerder had been busy obtaining influence over the crown prince. Wöllner gave private lectures to the royal heir, imparting not only Rosicrucian esoterica but demonstrating his reforming zeal as a far-sighted and moderate political conservative, just the thing Frederick William thought he wanted. Attempting to buttress but partially modify the rigid but fragile Frederician system, Wöllner advocated liberalizing mercantilist policies by promoting free trade, abandoning royal monopolies, and adopting a paternalistic social policy to protect workers against the emerging manufacturing class. He also recommended turning serfs into peasant proprietors on royal domains and church lands and entertained the breakup of Junker estates to the benefit of the peasantry. These and other policies indicate not only an interest in the preservation of the monarchy and its prerogatives but an imaginative and, dare one say, "enlightened" sense of social responsibility.

Despite the importance he attached to secular reforms, Wöllner considered them secondary to a Rosicrucian program of rescuing Prussia from the irreligion cultivated by Frederick II and his ministers. Under the prior monarch, Prussia had become something of a center for irreligion, owing in no small part to Frederick's unconcealed agnosticism and refusal to attend church. In 1785, Wöllner presented to the crown prince a detailed ecclesiastical program to be implemented in the coming reign. In contrast to preceding policy and practice, Wöllner contended for the importance of public expressions of faith, arguing that religion was necessary to public morality. Thus he encouraged Frederick William to be ostentatious in practicing his faith. He also believed it imperative that government should guard the populace against dangers to its religious commitment, even though he opposed persecution of men for their

5. Ibid., 358.

religious opinions. His primary concern focused on restraining antireligious or rationalist propaganda. To this end, he urged the crown prince, upon ascending the throne, to appoint an "honest man" to direct the Department of Ecclesiastical Affairs. He drew for the king a portrait of just such a man; it was a portrait of Wöllner himself.

Although he had completed planning his program some three years before he attained the post, Wöllner only began to implement it in 1788 (Frederick William had ascended the throne in August 1786) when the Edict Concerning Religion was adopted to enforce orthodoxy among preachers. Next came the Edict of Censorship, adopted the same year to repress irreligious writings, followed in 1791 by the *Immediat-Examinations-Kommission*, with the intention of putting teeth in the earlier Edict Concerning Religion. An additional measure, the *Landeskatechismus* of 1792, was adopted as a guidebook to define what was in fact orthodox and what unorthodox.

Without going into detail on the fate of these programs, suffice it to say they achieved only mixed results. Part of the problem, if problem it was, can be traced to Wöllner's humane and moderate nature, as well as to the incompetence of his subordinates. Though serious about the reforms, Wöllner was no Savonarola. And though a system of spies was eventually set up to keep an eye on the orthodoxy of clergy, theology professors, and schoolteachers, the system was far less sinister than it might sound. "A specific new set of preaching instructions," observes Epstein in detailing one of the measures, "required preachers to show their true colors (or become hypocrites) by preaching on assigned Biblical texts on specified Sundays, thereby ending the prevalent neological practice of avoiding those parts of the Bible which dealt with miracles, the incarnation, and other parts of orthodox dogma of which they disapproved."[6] In addition, all new candidates for ordination were required to sign a written pledge to preach only in accordance with the Augsburg Confession, followed by an oath of orthodoxy to be imposed on all Lutheran clergy.

6. Ibid., 364.

Although the strategy encouraged a measure of hypocrisy and opportunism in clerical circles, it succeeded in silencing the leaders of the Prussian *Aufklärung* as long as Wöllner had the support of the king. Support came to an end, however, when Wöllner received an unfavorable cabinet order in March 1794, deploring slow progress against proponents of Rationalism. He was subsequently fired from his position in the Building Department, an office he had continued to hold despite promotion to the Ecclesiastical Department, to allow him to give undivided attention to the religious struggle. In the event, Wöllner continued to urge a moderate policy, in opposition to the persecuting zeal of both his own subordinates and of Frederick William. He was never fully restored to the king's favor after this reprimand. By 1798, with a new king on the throne (Frederick William III), he was ungraciously dismissed from office without pension. He spent his remaining years as a discouraged landlord, on the estate he had purchased with his wife's money in 1790. He died in 1800, depressed and embittered by the treatment he had received.

Leaving eighteenth century Prussia behind, we turn our attention to the Netherlands a century hence, where the supremely gifted Abraham Kuyper (1837–1920) left an enduring legacy. As theologian, politician, and formative influence on neo-Calvinism, this dynamic reformer launched a daily newspaper, founded the Free University of Amsterdam, organized the Antirevolutionary Party (to combat the still potent ideas of the French Revolution), led a breakaway movement from the Dutch Reformed Church, and served as Prime Minister of the Netherlands from 1901 to 1905. In these endeavors, he acted in the spirit of his predecessor, Guillaume Groen Van Prinsterer (1801–1876), the aristocratic politician and historian who led both an evangelical revival (*Réveil*) and the antirevolutionary parliamentary caucus. Groen also wrote the influential *Unbelief and Revolution: A Series of Historical Lectures*, first published in 1847, which claimed that terminating Christianity in public life would lead to continuous political revolution, with the same baleful results as occurred during the French Revolution and its aftermath.

Attracted to such views, Kuyper abandoned his early flirtations with modernism and became a staunch defender of Calvinist orthodoxy. Yet his "neo-Calvinist" ideas—for all their traditional rigor

Tradition in the Protestant World

and passion—were perhaps influenced less by Groen or even Calvin himself than by Franz von Baader, Christian theosophist and German Catholic theologian and philosopher. "He is a mighty personality," Kuyper wrote of this Bavarian esotericist, "from whose mind flows a unique current of thought that has already watered every field of learning with its nurturing stream. His school is not theological but global . . . [and] cosmological. . . . [T]here is no better counterweight to the thinness of Modernism."[7] Drawing on Baader's theosophy, Kuyper wove into his Calvinist system such major concepts as religious antithesis, social organicism, sphere sovereignty, the centrality of the "heart," and opposition to the autonomy of theoretical thought.[8] In turn, these concepts greatly influenced Herman Dooyeweerd (1894–1977), who continued the Kuyperian stream in Dutch thought.

A second surprising source in Kuyper's formation arrived in the form of a present from his fiancée, Johanna Schaay. It was a copy of *The Heir of Redclyffe* (1853), written by the English novelist Charlotte Yonge under the sacramental, high church influence of John Henry Newman and the Oxford Movement. Though miles apart from Kuyper's eventual theological position, it left him with a love of Anglicanism's identity as a "mother-church" guiding each step of her pilgrims' spiritual journeys. The impact of the book, he said, helped free him from worldly ambitions and convinced him that the ministry, instead of a second-rate career, could lead many to salvation.

Following service in two parishes and the firming up of his Calvinist traditionalism, Kuyper took emeritation from formal ministry in 1874 and entered the political sphere, though retaining a seat as an elder on the Amsterdam consistory. "From there," according to historian James D. Braat, "he helped organize a national network to build up the ranks of the orthodox in pulpit and council room."[9] With the energy of ten men, he also began publication of a daily

7. James D. Bratt, ed. *Abraham Kuyper: A Centennial Reader* (Grand Rapids, MI: Wm. B. Eerdmans Publishing Co., 1998), 102.

8. J. Glenn Friesen, *Neo-Calvinism and Christian Theosophy: Franz von Baader, Abraham Kuyper, Herman Dooyeweerd* (Calgary, Alberta, Canada: Aevum Books, 2015), 81.

9. Bratt, *Abraham Kuyper*, 11.

newspaper (*De Standaard*), organized a national Anti-School Law League, frequently took to the floor of the Second Chamber to argue his causes "with facts and fancy oratory,"[10] founded a permanent organization to build a separate system of Christian elementary schools, created an association for Reformed higher education, and, in 1879, founded the Antirevolutionary Party (ARP) as an umbrella organization for his many endeavors. As an "antirevolutionary," Kuyper voiced objections to three principal things about the French Revolution and the spirit of 1789: they displaced divine transcendent authority with human rational authority; they substituted ideological schemes for patterns of organic historical development; and they "shattered social bonds by valorizing the individual and the ethics of self-interest."[11] In 1880, he founded the Free University of Amsterdam, a project at the heart of his dreams and one that would answer to each of his many callings. At its dedication, he famously declared "there is not a square inch in the whole domain of our human existence over which Christ, who is Sovereign over *all*, does not cry: 'Mine!'"

In 1886, Kuyper led an exodus from the state-sponsored Dutch Reformed Church. The move had its origin in the insistence of Kuyper and the Amsterdam Consistory that both clergy and church members be required to subscribe to the relevant Reformed confessions. Predictably, church liberals opposed any such requirement. Not only did the initiative fail, then, but Kuyper and eighty other members of the consistory were suspended. When their appeal was rejected by the provincial synod, Kuyper publicly addressed his followers in deep sorrow over the condition of the state church, after which he led the *Doleantie* (the "grieving ones") in the founding of a new church. By 1889, this new body—the Reformed Churches in the Netherlands—counted over two-hundred congregations and 180,000 members.

In the political sphere, in which Kuyper was leader of the ARP, he worked diligently to extend the franchise, realizing that the more the "little people" could vote, the better the orthodox cause would fare.

10. Ibid., 12.
11. Ibid., 13.

His support for franchise extension was principled as well as practical, and in the 1890s he spoke passionately on behalf of social democratic reforms. Though his policies eventually led to a split in the party, the division brought him back into office as a member of the Second Chamber in 1894. A mere seven years later, he became prime minister in the second Antirevolutionary-Catholic cabinet. Though his four years at the top were not a great success, his design of a coalition with Catholic support—that is, in alliance with Calvinism's age-old enemy—was a strategic masterstroke. He had worked to this end for some years with Herman Schaepman, a Catholic priest, politician, and poet whose antirevolutionary sentiments made him an ally of Kuyper. According to James Braat, "Kuyper knew confessors of Christ when he saw them, knew that Catholics qualified and that liberal humanists did not, their Protestant pedigree notwithstanding."[12]

Kuyper, whose Free University still thrives and whose example on various fronts is emulated by churches and educational institutions to this day in both the Netherlands and the United States, was more successful in his mission than was Johann Christoph von Wöllner in his. Yet both stand as capable and resolute opponents of 1789 and all that has issued from that watershed year. Moreover, they represent strands of character and doctrine clearly visible in our discussion of Maistre. Indeed, the political and social conservatism, the orthodox religious principles, and the esotericist inclinations make of them Protestant counterparts not only to Maistre but to Guénon, despite unavoidable differences owing to time, place, and personal foibles. For reasons such as these, they too stand as intriguing figures in the never-ending struggle against the humanist heterodoxy that blights so much of today's moral and cultural scene.

12. Ibid.

Bibliography

Armenteros, Carolina. *The French Idea of History: Joseph de Maistre and His Heirs, 1794–1854.* Ithaca and London: Cornell University Press, 2011.

Armenteros, Carolina and Richard A. Lebrun, eds. *Joseph de Maistre and the Legacy of Enlightenment.* University of Oxford: Voltaire Foundation, 2011.

Berlin, Isaiah. *The Crooked Timber of Humanity: Chapters in the History of Ideas.* Princeton, NJ: Princeton University Press, 1990.

Bolton, Robert. *Foundations of Free Will.* San Rafael, CA: Sophia Perennis, 2010.

———. *Keys of Gnosis.* Hillsdale, NY: Sophia Perennis, 2004.

Bradley, Owen. *A Modern Maistre: The Social & Political Thought of Joseph de Maistre.* Lincoln and London: University of Nebraska Press, 1999.

Bratt, James D., ed. *Abraham Kuyper: A Centennial Reader.* Grand Rapids, MI: Wm. B. Eerdmans Publishing Co., 1998.

Camcastle, Cara. Review of *Joseph de Maistre's Life, Thought, and Influence: Selected Studies,* ed. Richard A. Lebrun (Montreal-Kingston: McGill-Queen's University Press, 2001), www.firstprinciplesjournal.com (Spring, 2006).

Chacornac, Paul. *The Simple Life of René Guénon.* Hillsdale, NY: Sophia Perennis, 2004.

Cudworth, Ralph. *The True Intellectual System of the Universe, Wherein All the Reason and Philosophy of Atheism is Confuted and Its Impossibility Demonstrated,* 3 vols. London: Thomas Tegg, 1845.

Durant, Will. *The Story of Philosophy.* Garden City, NY: Garden City Publishing Co., Inc., 1933.

Epstein, Klaus. *The Genesis of German Conservatism.* Princeton, NJ: Princeton University Press, 1966.

Faivre, Antoine, and Jacob Needleman, eds. *Modern Esoteric Spirituality.* Vol. 21, *World Spirituality.* New York: The Crossroad Publishing Company, 1995.

Faivre, Antoine. *Access to Western Esotericism.* Albany: State University of New York Press, 1994.

————. *Theosophy, Imagination, Tradition: Studies in Western Esotericism*. Albany: State University of New York Press, 2000.

Friesen, J. Glenn. *Neo-Calvinism and Christian Theosophy: Franz von Baader, Abraham Kuyper, Herman Dooyeweerd*. Calgary, Alberta, Canada: Aevum Books, 2015.

Guénon, René. *East and West*. Ghent, NY: Sophia Perennis, 2001.

————. *Fundamental Symbols: The Universal Language of Sacred Science*. Cambridge, UK: Quinta Essentia, 1995.

————. *The Reign of Quantity and the Signs of the Times*. Ghent, NY: Sophia Perennis et Universalis, 1995.

————. *Spiritual Authority and Temporal Power*. Ghent, NY: Sophia Perennis, 2001.

————. *Studies in Freemasonry & the Compagnonnage*. San Rafael, CA: Sophia Perennis, 2004.

Hamilton, Alexander, James Madison and John Jay. *The Federalist Papers*. New York: A Mentor Book, The New American Library of World Literature, Inc., 1961.

Isham, Thomas Garrett. *Dimensions of the Enneagram: Triad, Tradition, Transformation*. Marshall, MI: The Lion and the Bee, 2004.

Kirk, Russell. *The Roots of American Order*. La Salle, IL: Open Court Publishing, 1975.

Lebrun, Richard A., *Joseph de Maistre: An Intellectual Militant*. Kingston and Montreal: McGill-Queen's University Press, 1988.

————. trans. and ed., *Maistre Studies*. Lanham, MD, New York, London: University Press of America, 1988.

————. *Throne and Altar: The Political and Religious Thought of Joseph de Maistre*. Ottawa, Canada: University of Ottawa Press, 1965.

Lewis, C. S., *Mere Christianity*. New York: Macmillan Publishing Co., Inc., 1976.

Lively, Jack, trans., *The Works of Joseph de Maistre*. New York: The Macmillan Company, 1965.

Maistre, Joseph de, *Against Rousseau: "On the State of Nature" and "On the Sovereignty of the People."* Translated by Richard A. Lebrun. Montreal & Kingston, London, Buffalo: McGill-Queen's University Press, 1996.

————. *An Examination of the Philosophy of Bacon: Wherein Different Questions of Rational Philosophy are Treated*. Translated and edited by Richard A. Lebrun. Montreal & Kingston, London, Buffalo: McGill-Queen's University Press, 1998.

————. *Considerations on France*. Translated and edited by Richard A.

Bibliography

Lebrun. Cambridge University Press, 1994.

———. *St Petersburg Dialogues: Or Conversations on the Temporal Government of Providence*. Translated and edited by Richard A. Lebrun. Montreal & Kingston, London, Buffalo: McGill-Queen's University Press, 1993.

Saint-Martin, Louis Claude de. *Theosophic Correspondence, 1792–1797*. Pasadena, CA: Theosophical University Press, 1991.

Van Dyke, Harry, trans. and ed. *Groen Van Prinsterer's Lectures on Unbelief and Revolution*. Ontario, Canada: Wedge Publishing Foundation, 1989.

Von Kuehnelt-Leddihn, Erik. *Leftism: From de Sade and Marx to Hitler and Marcuse*. New Rochelle, NY: Arlington House Publishers, 1974.

Waterfield, Robin, *René Guénon and the Future of the West*. San Rafael, CA: Sophia Perennis, 2002.

Index of Names

Adams, John, 82–83
Adams, John Quincy, 85–86
Alexander I, 16–17
Anizan, Jean-Emile, 20
Aquinas, Thomas, 97
Augustine, 26, 57

Baader, Franz von, 133
Bacon, Francis, 47–52
Bailly, Jean Sylvain, 59
Baudelaire, Charles, 104
Beauregard, Marquise Costa de, 30
Bergson, Henri, 121
Berkeley, George, 122
Berlin, Isaiah, 8, 84, 119–25
Bischoffwerder, Rudolph von, 128–30
Blavatsky, Madame, 21
Böhme, Jacob, 27, 32
Bonald, Louis de, 105, 119
Borella, Jean, 22
Bossuet, Jacques Benigne, 26
Bourignon, Antoinette, 27
Bray, Count de, 73
Brownson, Orestes, 85
Burke, Edmund, 3, 61, 80–81, 105, 127
Burnet, Gilbert, 83

Calvin, John, 72–73
Charles Duke of Courland, 128
Charles-Felix, 16
Chateaubriand, François-René de, 121
Cicero, 26
Cioran, E. M., 9

Clement of Alexandria, 33, 104
Clement of Rome, 34
Clement V, 98
Coke, Edward, 83
Coleridge, Samuel Taylor, 105
Condillac, Étienne de, 57, 86
Condorcet, Nicolas de, 81
Costa, Madame de, 106
Cracraft, James, 123
Cudworth, Ralph, 26, 47, 56–57, 77, 103

Dante, 96, 98
David, king of Israel, 68
Democritus, 52
Demotz (grandfather), 14
Descartes. René, 26, 48, 51–52, 57, 103
Dewey, John, 79
Dina, Marie, 20
Dionysius the Areopagite, 104
Dooyeweerd, Herman, 133
Duru, Madame, 18–20
Dutoit-Membrini, Jean-Philippe, 27

Eckartshausen, Karl von, 27
Epictetus, 55
Epicurus, 51–52
Etoles, Vignet des, 42

Fénelon, François, 26–27, 103
Ferdinand of Brunswick, 36, 40
Ficino, Marsilio, 2
Françoise (niece of R. Guénon), 19
Frederick II ("The Great"), 127–

29
Frederick William II, 127–32
Frederick William III, 130
Franklin, Benjamin, 82

Gentz, Friedrich, 81
George III, 28, 80
Giraud, Sebastien, 29, 39
Groen van Prinsterer, Guillaume, 105, 132–33
Guénon, Berthe (Loury), 19
Guénon, Fatima, 21
Guyon, Madame, 27–29

Haller, Karl von, 105
Hamilton, Alexander, 84
Harrington, James, 83
Hegel, Georg Wilhelm Friedrich, 122
Henry VIII, 99
Hoadly, Benjamin, 83
Hugo, Victor, 121
Hume, David, 111

Ibrahim, Muhammad, 21
Ignatius of Loyola, 11
Innocent X, 11
Itzenplitz, August Friedrich von, 129

James, William, 79, 97
Jansen, Cornelius, 11
Jefferson, Thomas, 82–83
Jesus Christ, 34, 134
Jung-Stilling, Johann H., 27

Kames, Lord, 83
Kant, Immanuel, 86, 122, 127
Kirchberger, Niklaus Anton, 27
Kirk, Russell, 80–81, 83
Kuyper, Abraham, 105, 127–35

Kuyper, Johanna (Schaay), 133

Lalande, Jérôme, 28
Lamennais, Hugues de, 104
Laski, Harold, 84
Lavater, Johann Caspar, 27
Law, William, 31–32
Leibnitz, Gottfried, 26, 57, 103
Lenin, Vladimir, 121
Lévi, Eliphas, 1
Lévi, Sylvain, 21
Lewis, C. S., 111
Locke, John, 49, 51, 57, 83, 86
Louis XIV, 99
Louis XVI, 58, 115
Luther, Martin, 72–73, 99

Maistre, André de (grandfather), 10
Maistre, Christine de (mother), 12
Maistre, Françoise de (wife), 15
Maistre, François-Xavier de (father), 10, 12
Maistre, Rudolphe de (son), 16
Maistre, Xavier de (brother), 16
Malebranche, Nicolas, 26, 86
Maritain, Jacques, 20
Marsais, Saint-Georges de, 27
Marx, Karl, 121
Maurras, Charles, 121
Mesmer, Friedrich, 39
Michelet, Jules, 121
Milhaud, M., 20
Mill, John Stuart, 122
Milton, John, 83
"Mirabeau," Honoré Riqueti, count of, 59
Mirandola, Giovanni Pico Della, 2
Montaigne, Michel de, 110

Index

More, Henry, 57
Möser, Friedrich von, 105
Moses, 50
Matter, Jacques, 1
Müller, Adam, 105
Münter, Friedrich, 39

Napoleon I, 15, 60
Neville, Henry, 83
Newman, John Henry, 133

Omodeo, A., 66
Origen, 26, 32, 57, 63, 76, 104
Ossellin, 54

Paine, Thomas, 81
Paracelsus, 49
Pascal, Blaise, 11, 103
Pasqually, Martinès de, 36
Péguy, Charles, 121
Peillaube, Émile, 20
Petau, Denis, 85
Philip the Fair, 97
Pius XI, 91
Place, M. de, 65
Plato, 5, 26, 34, 51, 57, 68, 103, 107, 122
Plutarch, 85
Prince Henry, 129
Pythagoras, 26

Rawls, John, 79
Rémusat, Charles de, 66
Renan, Ernest, 104
Revoire, Marc, 29
Robespierre, Maximilien, 58–59
Rohden, J. P., 66
Rorty, Richard, 79
Rousseau, Jean-Jacques, 47, 53–56, 81, 121
Russell, Bertrand, 122

St. Benedict, 60
Saint-Beuve, 48, 119
St. John, 60
St. Luke, 34
St. Martin, 60
Saint-Martin, Claude de, 25, 27, 31–32, 36, 45
Sales, Francis de, 11–12, 103
Schaepman, Herman, 135
Sertillanges, Antonin-Gilbert, 20
Sidney, Philip, 83
Smith, William, 82
Sorel, Georges, 121
Speranski, Michael, 17
Staël, Madame de, 15
Steuco, Agostino, 2
Swetchine, Madame, 67

Teresa of Avila, 27
Thouret, Jacques, 59
Tolstoy, Leo, 121
Trevor, John, 28
Trilling, Lionel, 87
Turgot, Ann Robert Jacques, 81

Victor Amadeus III, 14
Victor Emmanuel I, 15, 17
Vidalot, A., 66
Voltaire, 13, 15, 47, 53–54, 56, 66, 121

Washington, George, 82
Whitehead, Alfred North, 5
Wöllner, Johann Christoph, 105, 127–35
Willermoz, Jean-Baptiste, 35–38, 40–41

Yonge, Charlotte, 133

www.ingramcontent.com/pod-product-compliance
Lightning Source LLC
Chambersburg PA
CBHW021506090426
42739CB00007B/488